Upper Navigable Hudson River

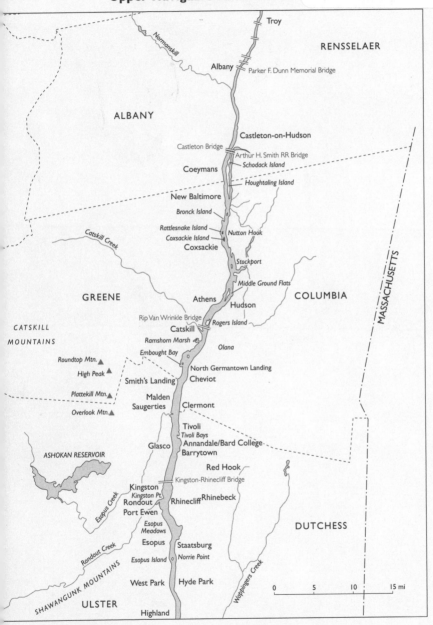

Troy

RENSSELAER

Normanskill

Albany — Parker F. Dunn Memorial Bridge

ALBANY

Castleton-on-Hudson
Castleton Bridge
Arthur H. Smith RR Bridge
Coeymans — Schodack Island

Houghtaling Island

New Baltimore
Bronck Island
Rattlesnake Island — Nutton Hook
Catskill Creek
Coxsackie Island
Coxsackie

Stockport

Middle Ground Flats

GREENE
Athens
COLUMBIA
Hudson
Rip Van Wrinkle Bridge — Rogers Island
CATSKILL
Catskill
MOUNTAINS
Ramshorn Marsh
Olana
Embought Bay
Roundtop Mtn.
North Germantown Landing
High Peak
Smith's Landing
Cheviot
Plattekill Mtn.
Malden
Overlook Mtn.
Saugerties
Clermont

ASHOKAN RESERVOIR
Tivoli
Tivoli Bays
Glasco
Annandale/Bard College
Barrytown

Red Hook

Kingston-Rhinecliff Bridge
Kingston
Kingston Pt.
Rondout
Rhinecliff Rhinebeck
Port Ewen

Esopus Creek
DUTCHESS
Esopus
Meadows
Esopus
Staatsburg
Rondout Creek
Esopus Island
Norrie Point

SHAWANGUNK MOUNTAINS
West Park
Hyde Park
Wappingers Creek
ULSTER
Highland

MASSACHUSETTS

0   5   10   15 mi

MY REACH

MY REACH

A HUDSON RIVER MEMOIR

SUSAN FOX ROGERS

Susan Fox Rogers

CORNELL UNIVERSITY PRESS
ITHACA AND LONDON

This publication was made possible, in part, through the generous support of a Faculty Research Grant from Bard College.

First published 2011 by Cornell University Press
Printed in the United States of America

Library of Congress Cataloging-in-Publication Data

Rogers, Susan Fox.
    My reach: a Hudson River memoir/Susan Fox Rogers.
        p. cm.
    Includes bibliographical references.
    ISBN 978-0-8014-5007-5 (cloth: alk. paper)
    1. Hudson River (N.Y. and N.J.)—Description and
travel.   2. Rogers, Susan Fox—Travel—Hudson River
(N.Y. and N.J.)   I. Title.
    F127.H8R64 2011
    974.7′3—dc22   2011012919

Cornell University Press strives to use environmentally responsible suppliers and materials to the fullest extent possible in the publishing of its books. Such materials include vegetable-based, low-VOC inks and acid-free papers that are recycled, totally chlorine-free, or partly composed of nonwood fibers. For further information, visit our website at www.cornellpress.cornell.edu.

Cloth printing   10 9 8 7 6 5 4 3 2 1

This book is dedicated with love to the memory of my parents, Jacqueline and Thomas Rogers

CONTENTS

A NOTE TO THE READER

This book chronicles my time on the Hudson River from the fall of 2004 to the summer of 2007. I paddled with many people and met others on the river; some names have been changed in this narrative. Many aspects of the river have altered since my writing—graffiti has been painted over; crumbling houses have been renovated or torn down; secret spots where I camped are now posted with No Trespassing signs; and ragged landings have been redone with picnic tables. I have left details as I saw and experienced them. I feel that these changes are part of the beauty of the river.

Environmental issues touched on in this story—in particular the cleanup of PCBs and the regulation of Indian Point—continue to evolve. General Electric began dredging in the spring of 2009 and then stopped its efforts in the summer of 2010 as high levels of PCBs were detected downstream. The conversation about what will happen next is active.

There is much I have left out—the range of the Hudson is such that I could offer only a slice of history and natural history. I have worked to be as accurate as possible. Any mistakes are my own.

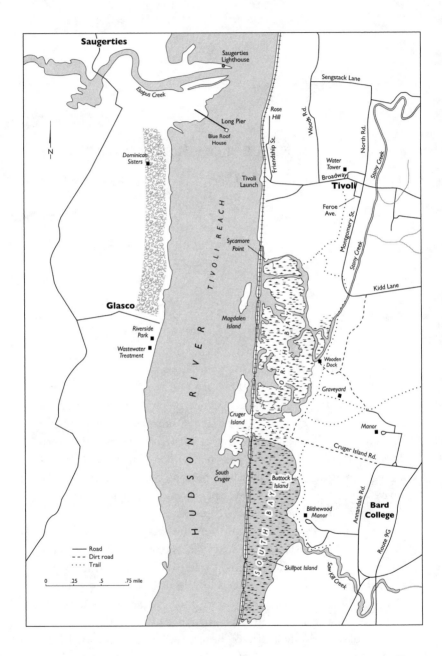

Saugerties

Saugerties
Lighthouse

Esopus Creek

Rose
Hill

Long Pier

Blue Roof
House

Sengstack Lane

Woods Rd.

North Rd.

Stony Creek

Dominican
Sisters

Friendship St.

Tivoli
Launch

Water
Tower

Broadway

Tivoli

Feroe
Ave.

Sycamore
Point

Montgomery St.

Stony Creek

Kidd Lane

Glasco

TIVOLI REACH

Magdalen
Island

Riverside
Park

Wastewater
Treatment

HUDSON RIVER

NORTH BAY

Wooden
Dock

Graveyard

Manor

Cruger
Island

Cruger Island Rd.

South
Cruger

Buttock
Island

Annandale Rd.

Bard
College

Blithewood
Manor

Route 9G

SOUTH BAY

Road
Dirt road
Trail

Skillpot Island

Saw Kill Creek

0   .25   .5   .75 mile

MY REACH

I

WHAT LINGERS

On a breezeless August day, white clouds hunched over the Catskill Mountains on the western shore of the Hudson River. A motorboat sped south, with a water-skier trailing behind. From a snag, a great blue heron launched, its body curved into a slim S-shape. Its wings beat strong and methodical, while its long legs drifted behind. Ring-billed gulls circled overhead. From shore, the metallic *tzi-tzi* of katydids filled the air. I pulled my visor down to shield my eyes from the reflection off the water. The bow of my kayak rocked from the wake of the motorboat; I leaned, in order to stay upright.

I had put my kayak into the water at the rugged launch in the village of Tivoli, 100 miles north of Manhattan. Moving against the current, I pointed north and soon passed the crumbling remains of the former train platform. The cement structure is a favorite local hangout. A few teenagers sat on the wall, legs dangling. Boys with bare torsos held beer cans in cozies. The smell of pot lingered in the air. One young woman raised a silent hand in hello. I released my paddle for a moment to wave back.

I hugged shore for a few hundred yards. There, a cement retaining wall flanks the eastern side of the railroad tracks. Built in 1914, it is about twenty feet high and is seemingly held together by nothing more than hope and some fat-lettered graffiti. In white paint the graffiti reads, *JANE LOVE'S HARRY.* The *y* in *Harry* snakes back under the whole long sentence to underline *love's. Love's.*

Above this wall sits Rose Hill, one of the many mansions that line the Hudson. It's a large, square, two-story brick house with a copper-brown roof. A porch with pillars lounges along the front, and toward the back a tower rises above the treetops. North of Rose Hill, I swung west to cross the river. In the middle of the deep shipping channel, I scanned north and south for a barge or tanker. The river behaved. That is, the wind did not pick up, as it so often did when I made this almost-daily crossing. My stroke even and slow, I could feel the current below me, ebbing toward the ocean with the outgoing tide.

Within twenty minutes I had reached the western shore, where the water was so shallow my paddle grazed the muddy bottom. Spatterdock covered the water's surface. A broad-leaved water plant, spatterdock drowns at high tide and sputters to the surface at low tide. Mid-June it puts out fat, yellow flowers.

I crossed the mouth of the Esopus Creek, a tributary of the Hudson, which drains the Catskill Mountains and spills out at Saugerties. The Esopus has a texture all its own, the water thicker, the air ripe with outboard-motor oil. I inhaled, enjoying the smell of a two-stroke engine. Near the channel that leads from the inland docks to the river, the water swirls into currents created by the movement of boats, the presence of submerged pylons, the force of a creek meeting a big river. The bow of my boat jostled as a small motorboat puttered by in front of me on its way out to the wide water.

I coasted north toward the Saugerties Lighthouse. Made of red brick with a sloping roof and a tall, square watchtower, the lighthouse looks like a house set on a round island. There's a stone and cement platform that rings the lighthouse. From the platform, a bridge spans fifteen feet to another drop of an island. At high tide, water flows under the bridge; on this day, the sandy riverbed emerged as the tide level dropped. The little island has a wooden deck and some benches shaded by two mulberry trees. It's a great place to picnic or to fish.

The original stone lighthouse, which operated with five whale-oil lamps, burned to the ground. The current one—one of seven left on the Hudson—was closed in 1954. After a few decades, the wear of neglect was evident, and a nonprofit organization formed in order to save it. Now an automated solar-powered white light flashes every four seconds from the forty-six-foot-tall tower. Since 1991 the building has served as a romantic bed-and-breakfast. A lighthouse keeper makes breakfast and from time to time opens the lighthouse for tours.

It seems an idyllic job—what a vantage from which to watch the world unfold. My envy dulled when I talked with a friend who was a recent keeper. In a flat, direct manner, Sasha Pearl said, "The best stories are the toilet stories." The toilet is a porta-potty installed on the dock for use by day visitors. It needs to be pumped out. A pump-out truck cannot make it down the three-quarter-mile footpath to the lighthouse. So the porta-potty needs to be moved. Sasha's job is to move the porta-potty on a trash barge, which is a raft with a motor kept afloat with insulation foam.

Since the porta-potty sits on a fixed-height dock, wrestling it onto the barge—"it's like moving a refrigerator"—needs to happen at the right moment in the tides. This is not necessarily high tide, as the rise and fall of the tide varies. So though she keeps a tide chart on the wall of the lighthouse kitchen, Sasha also waits up at night for the perfect moment when dock and barge align. "Two in the morning, three in the morning," she said, letting that fact of life sink in. The romance of being the lighthouse keeper is tempered further when she tells me of the time that the engine on the barge cut out. She was bringing in 2,000 pounds of coal, which is used to heat the lighthouse in the winter. She floated helplessly with her enormous load until a local boating friend rescued her.

Still, where Sasha gets to live is beautiful. On the first floor, the wide-board wooden floors are worn in both the kitchen area and the cozy living room. In a long room on the north side is a display of Hudson River and lighthouse memorabilia. There are great snippets of history here—from 1873 to 1885 the keeper was a woman, Kate

Crowley, who "kept a good light" and skated on the river in the winter. The second floor holds two light-filled bedrooms. A metal ladder leads to the lantern room and an outside platform. Views from this height extend north to the forested riverside, the town of Malden, and further on the stacks of the cement factories in Smith's Landing. To the south are Tivoli, and Magdalen and Cruger islands, and then 6.6 miles further south the Kingston-Rhinecliff Bridge spans the river.

On this August day, three adolescents stood on the far side of the little island under the shade of the mulberry trees. They held fishing poles in anticipation over the river. They kidded with each other as they tossed their lines into the water. Most people catch and release. From the gestures and bits of youthful taunting I heard, I sensed these kids were there for catch and torture. I suspected the worst because I know how awful kids can be, frying ants with magnifying glasses and exploding frogs with firecrackers.

As I rounded the little island to land on the beach on the north side, I heard the kids yelling, but not with pure excitement; disgust laced their cries. So I had to see what was going on. At the end of the fishing line wriggled an eel, about as long as my forearm but narrow, its sleek silver-black body shining in the sun. I couldn't watch what was going to happen next, so I paddled away. But the commotion didn't settle; when I turned and looked back, the eel was writhing in a shallow pool of water in that sandy slice of land between the lighthouse and the little island. A red gash shone where the hook had been torn from its mouth. I slid onto the beach and out of my boat. My intent was to scoop up the eel and toss it back into the river. The problem was, I was not so keen on touching the eel.

I have always been a bit fascinated and horrified by eels. They perform superfish feats such as moving across land. They can do this because they can breathe through their skin as well as through their gills. This is the sort of skill that might be celebrated, might make the eel a favorite among children. But eels do not fall into the charismatic creature category. They look too much like snakes (another marvelous and marvelously misunderstood creature), and the expression "slippery as an eel" is based in fact: they are particularly slimy. And they wriggle. In his wonderful, sadly out-of-print book *The Hudson River: A Natural and*

Unnatural History, Robert Boyle tells the story he heard of a gull that scooped up an eel. A few moments later, the gull started screaming; the eel pushed out of its anus and dropped back in the water. True story or not, it's a hard image to shake.

Given this creature's tenacity, I should have realized that the eel before me had a chance at survival. It would figure out how to move to safety. Still, I wanted to help.

"Here, use this," one of the kids said, bending over to hand me an empty Pringles can. His enormous jeans hung precariously below his hips.

I took the can, watched half of the eel disappear inside, and tried to scoop him up. No luck. He flopped back out, landing hard in his puddle. I realized I wasn't doing the eel any good. All three of the kids were now watching. I'm sure that to them I looked like what I was: a middle-aged woman fascinated by the wonders of the natural world. Or, more simply, they saw me as a nature lover, a tree hugger. What they could not see was that I wasn't just loving this eel. For the past several years I had been kayaking the Hudson, learning about this beautiful and ugly river. I had also been learning from the river. There is a lot to learn from any river, especially one as complicated as the Hudson. One thing I had come to understand was tenacity in all of its forms; living requires determination. Everything about the eel flopping in the puddle in front of us spoke to that resolve to live.

This eel had hatched in the Atlantic, in the warm waters of the Sargasso Sea, and over the course of a year had drifted in its larval form across the ocean, and up the river as a glass eel, a nearly transparent filament of life that could squirm in the palm of my hand. This movement from ocean to river, from salt to fresh or brackish water, defines the eel as catadromous, the only catadromous fish in North America. Eels swim in the waters from Greenland to Brazil, but this one had chosen the Hudson in which to mature. Perhaps it had huddled in one of the many tributaries along the river—the Saw Kill or Crum Elbow—growing longer and wider into a greenish-brown elver. It is at this stage that the eel is good for eating. The eel goes through one more stage of maturity, its yellow phase. Now it was silver-black and ready to breed, to head back out to the Sargasso Sea, which means it was at least three years old, maybe older. The whole life cycle is miraculous. And precarious. Eel populations are in decline for many reasons, including overfishing and dams that block their movement (though they can, at times, slither around dams). Scientists were lobbying to have the eel put on the endangered species list, an effort that failed in 2007. In any case, the survival of the eel was not being helped by kids with a fishing pole.

"Just pick him up," the girl said.

"No, you'll be electrocuted," one of the boys warned.

"No, I won't," I said. "We don't have electric eels in the Hudson." Still, I wasn't excited about reaching in and grabbing the eel.

"Then here, let me do it," said the boy who had given me the Pringles can. And then I realized that these kids, whose motives I had questioned, wanted to see the eel swim free as well.

"Don't do it," his friend warned. "You'll smell like eel for weeks. You can't get rid of the smell."

I crouched, made an open bowl with my hands, scooped under the eel, and flung him into the river. The residue of slime from his slick black body covered my hands. I stood and stared into the water, unable to see the eel as it swam off. Perhaps it would die from its wounds. But I hoped it swam south, carrying on its course of life. I cupped my hands to my nose to inhale the strong fishy smell that I hoped would linger for weeks, months, perhaps years.

2

MY REACH

One night, my first winter in Tivoli, snow fell in sheets. Near midnight, the Majer sisters, Emily and Carrie, threw snowballs at my house. The thunk against the gray vinyl siding woke me. I peered out the window at the dazzling snow. They beckoned to me with whistles and hoots. I dressed in layers to venture outside and join them.

The first big snowstorm of the season had roused the village, and out on Broadway, the streets buzzed with people shoveling snow. In front of the Black Swan, the only bar in town, drinkers were waging a snowball fight from one side of the street to the other, using parked cars as shields. An intrepid pickup truck swerved past us. A cord twenty feet long trailed from the truck, attached to a fat inner tube. On it were perched two women, clinging to the tube as it slid on the new snow. The truck turned onto Woods Road, and the tube swung out wide. The women's laughter echoed through the cold night air.

We walked in the middle of the street, a mile down the hill to the edge of town, as if pulled to the frozen river. There, the snow-flecked sky hovered all the darker for the luminescence of the jagged ice. We stood for a while on shore, tossing snowballs into the void. Emily's dog, Duck, barked in excitement, while we all laughed at nothing. Then we dragged ourselves away, trudged back uphill toward the lights of town. Several cars skidded, stalled, needed a push. We arrived on level ground, red-faced and exhilarated.

Through that winter, I made daily walks to the water's edge to watch the river in its frozen state. In the middle, a channel remained open, cut by a Coast Guard icebreaker. At times, a barge would knock its way through the chunks of ice. It sounded like someone crunching ice cubes, the noise amplified as if a microphone were pressed to her teeth. The air rattled for miles as the ship made its lonely journey north or south. Otherwise, the river was empty. Chunks of ice rose in crystal formation, almost inviting me to walk out. But the ice did not look thick enough to trust with my weight. I could not imagine how lighthouse keeper Kate Crowley, "who kept a good light," had once skated on this ice that offered few smooth surfaces.

In the early warm days of spring the river transformed as the ice began to move. Plates of ice clustered near shore. Further out, small bergs flowed north, and six hours later flowed back south with the tide. With my feet on solid ground, I enjoyed a sense of safety, watching this beautiful, dangerous world.

By late spring, I was done with being an admirer on shore. I wanted to be on the river. I found a used red plastic kayak for $650, bought a life jacket and a paddle, and strapped the boat to the top of my old Volvo. I drove west on Broadway, through the center of town with its post office and bakery, then veered downhill, passing two houses painted as color opposites: red with yellow trim and yellow with red, shaded by glorious weeping willows. At the bottom of the hill, a dozen houses line the riverfront.

A left turn onto Diana Street took me past a sign that reads Road Ends, though the asphalt continues up and over the railroad tracks. When a train approaches, red lights flash in warning and cantilevered bars lower to keep cars from crossing. Then the train roars through, blowing its whistle, shattering the waterfront peace. I have put pennies, nickels, and dimes on the tracks, but the train moves so fast that they are flung far into the gravel rail bed. I have never found one of my flattened coins.

Past the tracks is a small black dirt area where three cars can park. I pulled in beside a car with an empty kayak rack. Next to it, in a white Ford pickup truck, a man sat watching the river go by. Someone I guessed to be a student loitered by the river's edge, tossing stones. I walked over and asked, "Would you help me carry my boat?"

He nodded. "Of course."

It took me a few loads to get all of my gear together: spray skirt, life vest or PFD (personal flotation device), paddle, extra paddle, water, sunscreen. Then I stood on shore and scanned the water to see what the current was doing. I had not checked a tide chart, but I could tell that the tide was going out. The rocks up high were wet. The water level had dropped about two feet. I waded in, the cold gripping my calves. I stepped gingerly in my aqua socks, as the rocks were slick with a thin brown layer of silt, algae, and, at times, another oozy substance that did not feel natural.

Though I look at this launch with great affection—I am lucky to have a place to get across the tracks and to the river's edge—even I could see that this waterfront lacks charm. The Tivoli launch is but a few logs, drained of color, draped in front of large, square-cut rocks that mark the high waterline. At low tide, mud-slicked rocks send up a fermenting smell that is joined by the sharp odor of creosote from the railroad ties just yards away. On the east side of the tracks is an open space where CSX maintenance trucks park, adding an industrial ambiance to the setting.

I snapped the two sides of my breakdown paddle together, feathering them slightly. Then I slipped into my kayak and pulled the spray skirt tight, creating a seal that joined my boat and me. The molded plastic seat felt hard against my tailbone, as I sat with my legs bent, knees wedged against the braces. I dipped the yellow blade into the water and took my first stroke into the Hudson. I glided out, smooth on the calm water. I was alone under a light blue sky. The Catskills on the far shore cut a neat profile; a few cumulus clouds added texture to the scene but no threat of weather.

Though I had spent a lifetime outdoors rock climbing, cross-country skiing, biking, and hiking, I knew little about kayaks or the world of boats. I had been in a kayak a few times. I knew to place my hands shoulder width apart on the shaft of the paddle, and with little grace could manage to turn. But I did not know the finer details of how to paddle efficiently or any strokes beyond the basics. Still, paddling is like running: anyone can do it. To run or paddle well requires training and grace, but to put one foot in front of the other, to stick the paddle into the water and pull, is easy. That is what I did.

That spring day, the water colder than the air, I aimed for the nearest structure that called to me: the house with the blue metal roof at the end of a long pier on the opposite side of the river in Ulster County. I clutched my paddle too tightly as I stroked across the river. Once into calmer waters, in a little bay south of the house, I leaned into the hard seat and stretched my legs. With a splash of adrenalin, the world looked sparkly, and above me the sky unfolded wide. That first small excursion led to many more, and longer ones. My time on the water was freedom. And hope. I returned from my outings happy.

◊ ◊ ◊

I felt an urgency to know more, both about kayaking and about the river. I had long known some facts and history about the Hudson River. I knew it was an estuary and that the tides traveled the 154 miles from the Battery to the Troy Dam. In grade school, I learned of the key role the river played during the Revolution, and remembered the story of the chain strung across the river at West Point to stop British ships from traveling up the Hudson. I had studied the Hudson River School of painters in college, and was intrigued by the little people set in vast landscapes—that was so often how I felt. But the sunsets with swirls of orange and dramatic clouds in my opinion strayed too far from the real. I had read *Rip Van Winkle* and other Washington Irving tales, as well as Edith Wharton's *Hudson River Bracketed*. The title of the novel is an architectural style seen through the valley, one with "a hint of a steep roof, a jutting balcony, an aspiring turret." I was familiar with many of the environmental issues that arose from the battles on the river, particularly the pivotal Storm King case. History, natural history, art, literature, environmental issues—this was all rich material.

But these details were for everyone, could be learned sitting in a classroom. I sensed there were many, more intimate stories about the river. The life of the river I wanted to know would be found in exploring abandoned icehouses or cement factories that stand on the banks. Learning the river would mean seeing the sturgeon that course its depths, the snapping turtles and crabs lodged in the mud, and the osprey that plunge dramatically into the water as they hunt for food. If I wanted to know the river, I had to venture out.

I began my discoveries of the Hudson River in Tivoli, the village where I had recently bought a house. When I dropped my kayak in the water and looked back at shore, I saw a row of houses with open porches. The street that faced me, Friendship, was named by the Frenchman Pierre de Labigarre. In the 1790s he built his Chateau de Tivoli, and named the growing riverside community, then known as Red Hook Landing, Tivoli. He envisioned an American twin of the Italian town and planned the village streets with a utopian vision: Commerce, Plenty, and Peace. Up the hill, where I live, was a village named Myersville, then Mechanicsville, and finally Madalin; in 1872 the two communities united under the name of Tivoli. But de Labigarre was more of a dreamer than a planner; soon enough he ran out of money.

If the good Frenchman didn't manage to leave much in terms of street names or structures—his castle burned—he left his spirit. It can be found in locals who hope to win as they play bingo on Saturday nights or in Bard College graduates who never leave town, preferring country life over fast-paced careers. There's a handful of Manhattanites who garden so productively it looks like they are trying to remake the world. There are a few town drunks and a mustached man who wears camouflage and wanders the streets carrying a golf club. So though not everyone is sharing the same dream, still, Tivoli is filled with dreamers.

◊ ◊ ◊

In my kayak, I often head south out of Tivoli, sticking to the eastern shore, which takes me past a brick house named the Pynes, surrounded by towering white pine trees and one rounded copper beech. Not far south I get a glimpse of the sunflower-yellow private mansion named Callendar House, which dominates Sycamore Point. The white columns along the porch are like teeth grinning at the river. Both mansions were built shortly after the Revolution by members of the wealthy Livingston family, which dominated this section of the river. At the water's edge below Callendar House a stone dock, which was Hoffman's Landing, crumbles into the water. From there, ferry service ran to the western shore, and steamboats docked to gather and unload supplies. I swing out to avoid the remaining wood pylons, and blocks of cement that threaten to rip the bottom of my boat.

The strip of shoreline between the river's edge and the train tracks is narrow, but black willow, locust, and sumac trees intermix there with a range of shrubs, including the Eurasian buckthorn and ninebark. For some stretches, the growth is so dense I know the railroad is there only when a train thunders past, rocking the river bed, the water, and my soul.

My destination on most days is a gem of an island named Magdalen. The island appears to have a stone prow on the north end, and on the east side, a border mixed with rocks and sandy mud. The island is about 100 yards from shore, paralleling the train tracks. In this narrow divide between the railroad causeway and island the river bottom has silted in, and the water is shallow. Spatterdock grows thick, as does wild celery, which is a ribbonlike submerged vegetation. These plants tangle my paddles at low tide. In this protected, quiet side of the island I have seen many marvelous sights: a snapping turtle making its way toward shore, and at dusk one day thirty-two great egrets roosting, elongated white dots speckling the tall trees.

On the western shore, facing Magdalen, sits the hamlet of Glasco, in Ulster County. Glass, produced inland, was carried to docks along the Glasco Turnpike, then shipped downriver. I can just make out the water treatment plant, on the shores of the river, and the town park. A large red barn, owned by the Ciarlante family, stands next to a boat ramp. The outside of the building tells some of the story of harvesting ice, then paving. Just north of town directly on the water is the home of a couple, Dock and Kate, who live by the tides of the river. I think of them watching over the river and feel a twinge of jealousy. I often saw Dock in his rowboat, taking long, graceful strokes.

At the southern edge of Magdalen, rocks trail out, and at low tide I have run aground. "It's good to give rocks a wide berth," one boating friend advised with a smile when I told him about scraping onto those rocks. The fluky waters at the end of the island keep me on edge as they jostle me about. On the western side of Magdalen, the rock bed of the island carves forty-one feet deep. Waves from passing boats slosh up, roiling the waters. I enjoy the thrill of dancing on these more complicated stretches. And then I am relieved to return near the calmer shore as I head back to the Tivoli landing.

In the distance, the water tower announces TIVOLI in blue, blocky letters. It has suffered, or been graced with, graffiti—bold markings that I wish I could make sense of. It stands just off the park in the middle of my little village of 1,200, and beckons me home.

◊ ◊ ◊

Like many Hudson River towns, Tivoli is divorced from the river that created it. We don't make our living from Hudson River traffic or industry, we don't organize our days by the tides, and we don't take the ferry to Saugerties. Our train stop closed in 1960. With Manhattan hovering 100 miles south, people worry that if the train station reopened, our little village would be ruined. City dwellers with too much money and looking for quaintness would spill into the four restaurants; real estate prices would rise even higher; our quirkiness would become homogenized.

This concern appears irrational once I'm on the river, where land with all of its busyness and rules feels far away. Snug in my boat, I take pleasure in the differences between land and water. On the river, there are no traffic lights to obey, no speed limits except near marinas (and these do not apply to me—I do not create a wake), and no fences to obstruct my path. The river does have its rules of navigation, but they do not control what I can do, or curtail my freedom to travel from one side of the river to the other, at night or in daylight, under railroad bridges or into shallow waters. On the water, I have miles of river all mine to explore.

I kid myself imagining I am exploring the river. Every piece of it is charted, photographed, known. One of my favorite maps is a swirl of colors that shows the contours of the bottom of the river. It took years to create this map, with boats sounding the depths as they traveled methodically back and forth across the water. If you look at the map and let your imagination wander, it is possible to see the outlines of hundreds of things buried on the bottom of the river. These sunken objects are old piers, anchors, cable crossings, and boats of all sizes.

In the early to mid-nineteenth century, when steamboats ruled the river, the owners competed in price and the captains in speed as they made their way from Manhattan to Albany and back. Disasters small and large accompany the tales of these races. One of the most famous involves the *Henry Clay* racing the *Armenia* from Albany south. After cutting their prices from a half dollar to twenty-five cents, the two boats set out on July 28, 1852, each claiming it would offer the faster ride. They lapped each other as they made stops in the cities of Hudson, Kingston, and Newburgh. The boats trembled and spewed smoke, terrifying the passengers. The *Henry Clay* had passed Yonkers when it caught fire and ran aground. Some passengers were saved— one rescued by a Newfoundland dog—but many died, including Maria Hawthorne, sister of the novelist Nathaniel Hawthorne, and Andrew Jackson Downing, the landscape architect credited with many beautiful lawns and gardens surrounding estates in the valley. Parts of the *Henry Clay* as well as of sister steamboats are disintegrating at the bottom of the river.

It is not just sunken boats that we know of in the river. Scientists working out of the Beacon Institute for Rivers and Estuaries as well as at Stevens Institute are putting sensors in the river for real-time monitoring. We'll soon know where fish sleep or eat, the speed of the wind that ruffles the surface of the water, and where the water is 65 degrees. Still, because I approach each bend or cove filled with curiosity and knowing that I'll see something—an eagle or a heron, a fish leaping into the air or a painted turtle sunning on a log—I retain an explorer's sense of discovery. *No one has ever seen this before,* I think. *No one has ever been here before.* The desire to be first is the explorer's malady; I was born much too late to hope to be the first at anything. But despite the facts, the urge persists. If I am the first, then what I see I can claim as mine.

◊ ◊ ◊

The first European to navigate up the river was the Englishman Henry Hudson, who sailed for the Dutch East India Company. He traveled up the Hudson in the *Half Moon* in 1609, his third voyage in search of a passage to the East. Of course he was not the first person to gaze on and use these waters. For centuries Native peoples had been eating fish from the river and using beaver pelts to ward off the cold winters. One group of these Native peoples, the Mohican, called the river the Muhheakunnuk (also often spelled Mahicanituk), popularly translated as the "river that runs both ways," or the "waters that are constantly in motion." Less poetically it is simply the "river of the Mohican." When I try to pronounce Muhheakunnuk those *h*'s and *k*'s emerge from my throat like the mud of the river itself. Hudson called it the North River, as opposed to the South River, which is now called the Delaware. The British asserted the name Hudson in 1664 as they claimed their right to the river.

Henry Hudson made it to modern-day Troy. For many, that 154-mile stretch of estuary is *the* Hudson. But the source of the river is 161 miles to the north at Lake Tear of the Clouds, a small tarn on the southwestern slope of Mt. Marcy in the Adirondacks. The upper river, which flows above the Troy dam, is very different from the lower river. And within these two distinct sections, the river varies in width and depth, in texture and spirit. To speak of the Hudson as one is impossible. There is greater accuracy in naming and describing a section. A section of a river is called a reach.

Reach, of course, is both noun and verb. Until I started to paddle, it was all verb—what I could reach for. This wasn't just the butter on the table or a lover's hand as we took a walk. I grew up rock climbing, and to a climber reach is important. On a climb, if a hold was out of my reach, I fell. What I enjoyed about kayaking is that though it involved many things I had yet to discover, it did not involve falling. By the time I started kayaking, I had taken enough falls.

On my navigational chart, reaches are named for the small towns and villages that rim the river: the Malden-on-Hudson Reach, the North Germantown Reach, the Barrytown Reach. Robert Juet, Hudson's mate, named the thirteen-mile stretch from what is now Wappinger Creek to Crum Elbow Point, two miles north of Poughkeepsie, the Long Reach. That name remains, one of the fourteen reaches designated by the Dutch explorers. The first was the Chip Rock Reach along the Palisades while the dangerous stretch in the Highlands was Martyr's Reach.

In *The Hudson*, written in 1939 as part of the Rivers of America series, Carl Carmer describes a range of reaches: "Hoge's and the high banks of Vorsen, Fisher's and the sweet-smelling Clover with the long high wail of mountain wildcats drifting over it. The Bacerack, Playsier—the almost endless waters of the Vast, and finally the jungle banks of Hunter's." This passage is pure Carmer, who describes—and often exaggerates—the wonder and romance of the river; his book remains one of the most lively and readable on the Hudson. But even without Carmer's help, the names of the reaches are evocative. A reach holds its own mystery.

When I slip my boat into the water off Tivoli, my gaze travels past the length of the Tivoli Reach—which is about a thousand yards long—and stretches south to Magdalen Island, and on to the larger Cruger Island. To the north my vision extends to where the river bends past the Saugerties Lighthouse. In this section of river, I anticipate the areas where submerged grasses grab my paddle, and I look forward to the eagle often perched on Cruger Island. At the southern end of Magdalen Island I adjust, anticipating the brisk current there. It took four years of dipping into these waters before I knew the names of the houses that line the river, and became acquainted with the rocks and tree limbs on shore. Over the years, I noted with pleasure the palette of the water as it morphed from light chocolate to the green brown of a dirty emerald. And I grinned at sunsets, from the tame to those that displayed a range of explosive oranges, stretching out from behind the Catskills. When I return to Tivoli, arms sore, I know, high or low tide, where the rocks stick out and how to maneuver in to miss them. There is still much to learn, but I know this section of the river well. I think of it as my reach, Rogers Reach.

As I paddled about, seemingly carefree, bringing this land and river into my body, memorizing its bends and currents, I knew I would need it, would need a solid, watery base to hold me in the coming years.

3

SWIMMING THE HUDSON

The Hudson River never looks clean. It's a turbid river. If you sink your hand into the water it will disappear into the murk. Add to that the flotsam—bottles and tires and plastic bags—that settles on shore after a storm-induced high tide, and it's a pretty unappealing place to swim. Still, I had an urge to swim to the other side. I let that urge marinate for a few years, and then in an impulsive moment told a student, Emmet Van Driesche, that I would work with him on his year-long senior project if he swam the Hudson with me.

Bard is a college with novel teacher-student relationships. Though I know that some of my colleagues or the administration might find a swim across the Hudson an unusual project requirement, Emmet did not blink. I knew he wouldn't. As a student, I would have thrilled at such a scheme, and I had come to see Emmet as a young version of myself. For the past two summers, Emmet had disappeared aboard tall sailing ships on the West Coast and returned in the fall speaking the language of knots and rigging, of tar and sails. I did the same at his age, only I went to Colorado, and then Yosemite to rock climb. I spoke the language of biners and nuts, of screamers and run-outs.

Whenever Emmet arrived at my office he smelled of the outdoors, and in warmer weather he was often carrying the canoe paddle he had whittled. Whether warm or cold outside, he wore the same outfit: Carhartts streaked with tar and a white tank top that revealed his round, tanned shoulders.

An outfit—a uniform—is important. It announces who you are, adds to your identity. My climbing clothes mattered—the blue-striped rugby shirt and white painter's pants said, as clearly as the carabiner dangling from my knapsack, that I was a climber. My teaching garb is a lot less imaginative: black shoes, pants, shirt, and jacket. I do not yet have a set of kayaking clothes, and I am not sure what that gear would look like. Boaters heading into cold waters wear either dry suits or wet suits, as I did in early spring and late fall. But the rest of the long summer I imagined the finest uniform to be tattered clothes, the sort that I would not mind getting wet if I decided to spill over into the water to cool off.

◊ ◊ ◊

When people learn that I spend days on the water, they don't ask about the history of Cruger Island or wonder about the sturgeon that prowl the waters. They ask, "Is it safe to swim?"

They do not fear the barges that might emerge from north or south and run them over. Rather, they are asking if the river is clean. If they swam the river, and took in a mouthful of water, what would they be swallowing? When I meet someone who has grown up near the river, he tells me that he was warned not to stick a foot in the river, not to touch the water, as if he could be poisoned on contact. Those early lessons are hard to shake.

I counter these worries with a revealing fact: Poughkeepsie, along with eight other communities along the river, takes its drinking water from the Hudson. Or this: there are now five official swimming areas along the river, with another thirteen sites targeted for development.

Or this: people swim around Manhattan. OK, tetanus shots are recommended, and some people become ill, but still, upriver must be cleaner than New York Harbor.

My arguments are futile in most cases. If a person sees the river as dirty, it's dirty. And that person is not entirely wrong. The cleanliness of the river varies. Those areas near a sewage treatment discharge pipe are obviously less clean, and, after a decent rainstorm, bacteria counts can climb to unhealthy levels. Oil spills that coat the river or sewage pipes that break are not uncommon events. The Clean Water Act of 1972 mandated clean water by 1985. We long ago missed that goal. But the river is cleaner, and a river invites crossing.

◊ ◊ ◊

Early September of 2004 Emmet appeared at my office door.

"When are we going to swim the Hudson?" He leaned against the doorjamb, smiling. It was a wicked smile, challenging and full of the glee.

I had spent a lot of time thinking about where to cross. A solid landing on both shores was important. Much of the shoreline is a thick ooze, often interwoven with a range of submerged vegetation. I did not want to tangle up in plants or have my feet sink into muck. On the eastern shore, landings are complicated by the rocks, called riprap, that support the railroad. Riprap is bordered by trees and bushes, which are often laced with poison ivy. Besides a good landing, the most important thing we needed was to be able to see into the distance, both north and south. We had to stay out of the way of big boats on the river—they couldn't swerve or slow. I scoped out many locations and ended up deciding the best was the half-mile crossing closest to home.

The following Friday morning Emmet showed up at the Tivoli landing with a canoe and a friend in a bikini. She had dark hair and a slight frame. I wondered if she knew what she had gotten herself into. In my mind, this was the sort of undertaking that needed more than a bikini.

Was this young woman a girlfriend? Just as students never imagine the faculty have a life beyond the campus, I do not think of my students beyond what they have written. I had known and worked with Emmet for some time yet had no idea if he was in a relationship. But I could imagine he had a girlfriend; Emmet is a good-looking boy, with a strong nose, clear brown eyes, and golden smooth skin framed by dark hair that looks like it will never fade or thin. He carries his confidence in his strong back and legs, and, from time to time, it flashes into a glorious arrogance. His assuredness might have intimidated me at eighteen; the older me found Emmet's boldness charming.

Girlfriend or not, Sarit was quiet but game. We stood on shore and considered our options. None of us had checked a weather report, but we were lucky: it was one of those perfect early fall days that foretold the cooler air to come. A few trees had started to show a tinge of red or yellow. The water was still summer-warmed.

We decided we would aim for the jetty called Long Pier, across the river and slightly to the north of us. The house with the blue roof that sat at the end of the jetty had been my first destination on the river, and it remained a good, clear point to navigate toward. Emmet would swim over, flanked by Sarit and me in boats, and she and I would swim the return. It was just past high tide, the water poised in that moment of seeming indecision called slack tide before it moves back out. Water covered most of the small landing, leaving exposed one long dead tree that had floated to shore.

I slipped into my kayak, and Sarit took Emmet's canoe. With two boats we had more of a chance of being visible. We waited for Emmet as he waded out waist deep, then dove in, whooping with delight. He varied his stroke, flipping from backstroke to crawl to breaststroke, dunking his head underwater.

I scanned north while Sarit kept an eye to the south. I would stroke, then lean back in my seat and let my kayak glide in the smooth water. On the far shore sat two large, white houses, one long, with a row of windows, the other with tall pillars. The one belongs to the Dominican Sisters, who own a mile of wooded shoreline from Long Pier south. The other house I have heard was once a sanitarium. In the distance Overlook Mountain rose steeply above the town of Woodstock, the fire tower on the summit barely visible. North of Overlook was the flat top of Plattekill Mountain, then a dip into the Plattekill Clove. Further north I could see the distinct summits of Kaaterskill High Peak and Roundtop, which reaches 3,440 feet above sea level. In the morning sunlight they looked like they were draped in a yellow-green carpet. In a few weeks the parade of fall colors would march up the flanks of the mountains.

A motorboat passed midriver, and a few minutes later the wake lifted the bow of my boat. Emmet took in a mouthful of water. He stopped to cough, then treaded to get a sense of where he had come from and where he was going.

"Not too much further," we encouraged. "Keep going." I did not want to loiter there, in the deepest section of the river, where the bottom drops to fifty feet. In these deeper sections, the water pulls harder. But it is also in the deep sections that boats move, especially the large tankers and tugs with barges. The deep section of the river is their domain.

Within half an hour we were on the western shore—about the same amount of time it took the ferry to make the crossing to Saugerties when it ran between 1859 and 1940. Emmet glowed with the fun of his river crossing. Sarit and I clambered out of our boats and onto the large rocks of the jetty. To the north we could see the Saugerties Lighthouse. At this rocky point, the water drops to twenty feet. Steamboats once docked here. Now, fishermen often anchor, their lines trailing into the depths. The privately owned red brick house with the blue roof sat empty, as it always seemed to be. It was a shame—perched at the end of a long breakwater, it stuck far into the river. I imagined sitting on the porch watching the river go by, or the morning sunlight flooding the long windows on the second floor.

I removed my T-shirt and stood in a one-piece bathing suit, aqua socks covering my feet. I didn't want to puncture my skin on anything sharp, like the hard spiky black water-chestnut seeds. And the river could offer up other unexpected sharp objects: a framing nail, a glass bottle, or a broken piece of hard plastic.

I stared out at the river from atop a large rock, while Emmet tied my kayak to the back of his canoe. The eastern shore looked further than I wanted it to be. The water and sky joined to expand the emptiness in three dimensions, dwarfing trees on the far shore. Even the white three-story wooden house with the long front porch on Friendship Street looked miniature.

"Well, here we go," I said, but there I was, feet still planted on shore. Setting myself afloat in so much water was daunting. I reasoned that at least I would always have an eye on both shores.

Sarit was also still on shore, laughing with me.

"OK, one, two, three." I coaxed, as my parents had when I was a child. Sarit stepped off her rock and sunk, then surfaced and started to swim with strong, confident strokes. I slid in, the warm water enveloping me. The texture of the water felt gritty against my skin, and I closed my mouth tight, breathing through my nose. I took my first strokes, moving into a crawl.

Swimming in open water is not swimming in a pool. Though the water looked calm, when I tilted my head to the side to take a gulp of air, water jostled into my mouth. The river was clean enough to swim, but I was not keen on swallowing any water. I could not do the crawl for a long stretch because even with goggles the murky water stunted my range of vision. So I swam like Tarzan, head above water, and when that became tiring, I flipped onto my back, stroked for a while, then righted myself to do the breaststroke.

Emmet sat high in his canoe and sang a classic work song. Sarit took the lead, to his right side, and I dangled back to the north. I stopped, hovering in the water, to look around, the Catskills to the west now huge. As the sun rose higher, a wind picked up, just enough to rustle the surface.

"You OK?" Emmet asked.

"Sure," I called back, though I felt a bit at sea, knocked around and small. The subtle outgoing current tugged at my legs.

Real breaststrokers bob and thrust with speed, but for most of us, the breaststroke holds little power. The breaststroke was my mother, Jacquie's, stroke. She loved to swim and did so daily in the local pool. But she enjoyed most swimming in the ocean, believing that a good dip could rid you of most any ache or malady. Her devoted swimming did not, however, translate into talent or skill. She swam slowly, very slowly—just as I did there in the middle of the river.

The chop of the Hudson reminded me of a day a dozen years ago when my mother and I were swimming in France, in the Bay of Biscay. She bobbed in the water near me, the waves sloshing us both around. Suddenly, I realized that we were being dragged out to sea by a strong current. "Hold on," I yelled, convinced I could do what everyone is told not to try: swim out of the riptide. She continued with her slow, ineffective stroke, while I frantically wore myself out. From time to time she let out a little laugh as we jostled further out to sea. Oblivious of the danger, she found this all rather fun, while I feared we were both going to drown. We were dragged out to sea and over 200 yards south. From shore, a lifeguard miraculously appeared at our sides, fins on his feet, a rope attached to the life vest he wore. He wrapped an arm around my mother, while I held his shoulder. He kicked while those on shore pulled us all in to safety.

I thought of my mother's unworried stroke through life, and my body relaxed against the small waves of the Hudson. I started to appreciate my turtle's perspective on the world. Everything—the houses on shore, the scraggly trees by the riverside, and the side of Emmet's canoe—looked oversized. And then there was something very big looming in the south.

"Swim a little faster," Emmet coaxed. "I see a barge."

I stopped to focus, to be sure he wasn't joking. The vision of the barge on the horizon made me feel like a butterfly in a stiff wind trying to dodge an oncoming car. My muscles became soft, my skin tender. The bottom of the river pulled at my toes. I plunged forward, fueled by adrenalin.

After our half-hour swim, we dragged up on shore, elated. While we were still drying off and congratulating ourselves, the barge swooshed by. *That was pretty stupid,* I thought. *But fun.*

I could make a long list of stupid but fun things I have done: hitch-hiked to Yosemite when I was nineteen; rock climbed naked (I arrived on the first belay ledge, and my partner at the time asked, "What were you thinking?"); bicycled through Central Park at two in the morning;

climbed a supporting wall to the West Side Highway in Manhattan; camped alone in Denali with a bivouac bag (the mosquitoes almost devoured me). And then there are the dozens of tales where I emerged from a hike or backcountry ski long past dark in the rain or snow, temperatures well below zero. I love these moments—although in the moment, when I think I might be lost or benighted, when the pain or cold is high, I'm not thinking fun, I'm thinking nothing. I'm just surviving, letting my animal instincts take over as I experience that essential and invigorating will to live.

◊ ◊ ◊

One summer when I was eight and my sister Becky was ten, we were floating on mattresses on a Cape Cod pond. Our father, Thomas, sat twenty feet away on the sandy shore, reading while keeping an eye on us. Turning lazily toward me, Becky said, "Susie, it's your duty to keep America beautiful."

Our father, not realizing Becky had taken this line from a television ad, loved her sincere tone, and this odd command that the beauty of America rested in my small hands. For years he repeated the line: "Susie, it's your duty to keep America beautiful." Then we would all laugh.

Becky and I were children in the 1960s in a college town—and all of those great movements of the era seeped in, to one degree or another. The basic lessons from the environmental movement at that time—turn off lights, pick up garbage—I listened to with great earnestness. Those lessons still apply—we still need to turn off lights and pick up trash. And so that is what I have done my whole life. Locally, I had joined the Red Hook Clean Up Day and dragged dozens of bags of trash off the sides of Dutchess County roads. My kayaking friend Carol Lewis and I have paddled out in canoes and hauled spent tires out of North Tivoli Bay, as well as a range of other stuff people toss overboard—dolls, coolers, Styrofoam, plastic jugs.

In the face of our environmental troubles, picking up trash is not much. Still, it's a piece. It's what I can do. This sort of one-woman, one-river, one-little-bit of work fits in with the philosophy of the environmental organization Clearwater. Since 1969, Clearwater has sailed a beautiful sloop on the river, bringing out young people and adults to sail, pull in fish, and discover the river. The thrill of hoisting sail, of seeing the world anew by floating on the water, changes those who spend time on the boat. Behind this grassroots vision is musician and activist Pete Seeger. So music is central to the work of Clearwater. Every spring it holds the Hudson River Revival, attracting hundreds who sing and enjoy the river.

Keeping a river clean takes constant work and vigilance. Clearwater has been attentive, but it is not alone. The pit bull of environmental groups on the river is Riverkeeper. It has a patrol boat, the *R. Ian Fletcher*, captained by John Lipscomb, who spends hundreds of hours every year on the river. "Just seeing the boat makes people think twice," John once told me. Twice about polluting. And if they don't think twice, Riverkeeper resorts to the instrument of choice: the law and our court system.

The other major nonprofit organization at work on the river is Scenic Hudson, which focuses on land preservation and the visual beauty of the river. Riverfront property is precious, so Scenic Hudson's work requires genius real estate skills and plenty of cash. It has opened much of the land it owns for public use, creating parks and trails that flank the river.

Of course, there are many other organizations at work, including local land trusts, New York State's Department of Environmental Conservation, and national groups with a local presence, like Audubon and the Nature Conservancy. And behind these groups there have been or are many people: Robert Kennedy, Jr., the late Franny Reese, Fran Dunwell, Robert Boyle, John Cronin. The list goes on for pages. There are a lot of strong personalities in this lineup, and those personalities often clash. Still, everyone is working toward the same thing, and that work is real. Despite many victories, no one is sitting back and relishing successes. As much as has been accomplished, an equal amount (or more) remains to be done. And I will continue to pick up garbage.

If the river was clean enough for Emmet, Sarit, and me to swim that fall day, it was thanks to the work of all of these organizations, the devotion of all of these people.

◊ ◊ ◊

"That was great," I said to my young friends. "Thank you."

Though our feat called for a celebratory stack of pancakes, we loaded the boats onto our cars and went our own ways.

That swim proved a few things: Emmet was game, and Emmet would show up. That's all I need in a traveling partner. So when in February of 2005 Emmet suggested that after graduation we paddle the Hudson from Tivoli to Manhattan, without hesitation I said yes.

4

COURAGE

I tightened my rain parka and stretched the spray skirt into position, joining my body to my boat. A steady rain wed with the cold of the river below me. Emmet, perched on a wicker seat high in his canoe, stroked out into the gloomy water with his hand-whittled paddle. It was Sunday, May 22, 2005, and we were 101 miles from our destination, the George Washington Bridge. I tucked in near shore in my slender kayak, my orange paddle cradled in my palms.

Emmet glided toward me, then pulled ahead.

"Since I'm twice as old, and my equipment twice as efficient, there is half a chance I can keep up with you," I called.

Emmet laughed. "This isn't a race."

The waves pushed me around. I thought, *We are off!* To what I did not know. In the rush of the end of the school year Emmet and I had not discussed logistics or scanned maps together, we had not divvied up gear. Two days before we left we agreed to go light—no stove—and that I would bring the peanut butter, he was in charge of jelly. We would both bring whatever snacks we wanted.

◊ ◊ ◊

My sense of adventure was keen, as I had spent six weeks in December and January in the Antarctic on a writer's grant from the National Science Foundation. Everyone I met on that cold, remote continent had big stories of exciting journeys, on and off the ice. I had returned intoxicated by the hope I found there, and promised myself I would spend more time in my tent. Before the Antarctic, I had been lulled by the business of middle age: working, paying a mortgage, and worrying over my parents. The previous fall my father had been hospitalized with pancreatitis and a few years before had had colon surgery. He now had to watch his exuberant diet and had given up drinking, though he still served a dry martini to friends who stopped by after work.

In anticipation of the trips I would take on the river, I had bought a new kayak, a sixteen-and-a-half-foot-long, forty-nine-pound red fiberglass Wilderness Systems Tempest, which the manufacturer describes as "friendly" and "forgiving." Before buying it I read up on boats. There was a range of hulls, those with hard chines versus more rounded bottoms, and this all meant something in terms of stability or the ability to roll. I took in information on length and width and how that affects the way a boat tracks through the water. Above all, website advice urged everyone to try out boats to see what fits, what works for your body type. They warned against falling in love with a boat. That is what I did.

I drove over to Kenco, an outdoor shop in Kingston, and was drawn to the shiny boat. I thought it beautiful, with long lines and a low deck. There were three hatches where I imagined storing my tent and stove. I could see its shallow V-hull would keep me close to the water. As I ran through all the reasons I had to own this boat, I told myself that at forty-nine pounds it was much lighter than my plastic boat, so it would be easier to get on and off the roof rack and into the water. But the logic of the purchase paled in comparison to the thrill I felt when

I sat in the boat on the showroom floor. I leaned into the padded seat that held me tight in the hips, and I imagined hours sitting there. I was wearing the kayak, the way I wear a pair of jeans or running shoes. It fit, my knees against the hull, my thighs in contact with the underside of the cockpit rim. Half an hour later, I pulled out my credit card. For good measure, I threw in an ultralight orange Werner paddle.

◊ ◊ ◊

Emmet and I moved through the familiar territory of my reach—Magdalen Island, brilliant green hovering above the turbid water, and the little hamlet of Glasco, barely visible on the far shore. We hugged the flank of Cruger Island, with wisteria and lilac in irresistible bloom. A strong wind at our backs scooted us along. Swells lifted my boat, and I surfed, letting the waves, which formed with the union of current and wind, carry me forward. Often, the waves took me by surprise, lifting the boat high and pushing my bow to the side. I worked with excitement and a touch of fear in order to ride with the wave, not get tumbled by it.

Past Cruger, South Tivoli Bay opens the sky wide. Above the bay, the white graduation tent staked on the Blithewood lawn at Bard College poked through the trees. The postgraduation dinner I'd attended under that tent was a day past and a world away. Then it was sunny, now it was raining; then I was in skirt and high heels, now I was in long pants and rain parka. I had spent graduation day greeting parents, congratulating everyone, and saying good-bye over and over again to students who had become the focus of my life. I would miss this class of students. They were the first that I had taught from first year to graduation; I'd watched them grow up. I knew some would send postcards from Montana or India and in the coming years ask for recommendations for graduate school or their first real job. They would e-mail asking, "Do you remember me from First Year Seminar?" and I would respond, "Of course." Some students, especially those who become writers and teachers, are friends. They write telling me how difficult grading is, and I laugh as I commiserate. But most of my students walk into the world, and I never hear from them again.

Emmet and I soon passed under the Kingston-Rhinecliff Bridge, and Emmet shrunk next to the pylons that soar to 152 feet. Bridges are sure markers, dividing the river on its north-and-south axis while connecting east with west. Most of the bridges have been built to duplicate long-used ferry routes, those places where people needed to cross from one town to another to share goods, news, friendship, or love.

Since I moved to this area in 2001, this bridge had been under repair. Stopped in traffic, I found the slow progress of the work tedious. I would sit and ponder over the green signs lining the bridge that proclaim, "Life is worth living." Would those words really help someone in despair? From below, however, the construction that straddled the soaring steel beams looked beautiful. Through the deep mist, the orange protective cover that draped the bridge was rather like a Christo wrapping. This wrapping, though, offers more than aesthetic pleasure. The bridge authority used to hose off the debris from the bridges, sending pounds of lead-based paint chips into the river. The wrapping now captures those paint chips.

After three hours of nonstop movement, Emmet and I coasted into the cement slip in Rhinecliff. It was two in the afternoon, but the light hadn't changed all day. The sky was so thick with clouds, I could not tell where the sun was. Water from the river, as well as the intermittent rain, had soaked the cockpit of my boat—I had not attached my spray skirt properly—and I wished I had a sponge to mop out my boat. My shoulders and lower back ached. We stretched while eating our first peanut butter and jelly sandwiches.

Across the river sat the Rondout Lighthouse, just off the city of Kingston. Though it already felt as if we were far from home, truth is, twenty-five minutes by car gets me from Tivoli to Rhinecliff. I was eager to keep moving into the unknown of this journey. That unknown is the reason I head out. From experience, I knew that wherever I ended up might not be beautiful, fun, or easy, but it would be wonderful. Wonderful, because I would be pulled from the everyday and awaken to a new landscape. My gaze would turn surely outward. That was the greatest pleasure. In that outward gaze, I could forget myself and my small and large worries. Perspective—that's what the natural world gives me.

For the next four days Emmet and I would return to the basics: eat, sleep, paddle. I love this simplicity. In it, I hoped to capture the magical sense of self-sufficiency that leads me to believe I can go anywhere, and do anything.

I needed that sense of strength. When I first started to dream of this trip, I did not know that in February my mother would begin to lose weight, and then her eyesight would fail; in March doctors would find several tumors in her brain; in April she would have surgery. We would later learn those brain tumors had originated in her lungs. By May she was enduring chemotherapy and radiation.

When doctors first found the tumors, my parents called from the parking lot of the Honey Creek Inn in Reedsville, Pennsylvania, on their way home from Hershey Medical Center.

"They found some growths," my father said, not able to use the word *tumor,* and far from the word *cancer.*

"Can I speak to her?" I hoped I could keep my voice steady. "How are you, little mother?" What I wanted to ask was, Are you frightened?

"I'm going to have the French toast for lunch," she said.

"That's great," was all I could say.

◊ ◊ ◊

Emmet and I packed up and continued south in the rain. I loitered for a while to watch a great blue heron, poised and still in the shallow waters. Then, without warning, it plunged, beak first into the water. There, speared at the end of the heron's long beak, was a fish flopping about. The heron stood, looking stunned in its own way, before flipping the fish into its beak. I saw the bulge of fish as it moved down the long, thin neck of the bird.

The solitary statuesque figures of great blue herons dot the riverbanks. They are so still, their wispy gray feathers blending with rocks and reeds, that I am often near before the outlines of the birds take shape. Their long beaks, with a sliver of orange, often let me know they are there before I discern their bodies.

Great blue herons are one of a few species whose population was not decimated by DDT, as were the osprey and eagle. They are a hardy bird; even with moderate levels of toxins, including PCBs in their system, they continue to hatch young that successfully fledge. Their populations are no longer in danger, as they were before 1900, when they were hunted for their feathers. These feathers were used in hats and, I have read, for cooking utensils. I have trouble imagining what I would cook that would require a heron feather. The Lacey Act of 1900 forbids the traffic of plants and animals, including feathers. That act, along with the 1918 Migratory Bird Treaty Act, helped to save the heron.

Though herons are not rare, every sighting is special. It is partly their striking elegance, but also their size—up to four feet tall with a wingspan of as much as five feet. That they are solitary creatures except when they roost, perching high in the trees, speaks to me.

◊ ◊ ◊

The water calmed as the sun attempted a last peek through the clouds that had blanketed us all day. We hugged the western shoreline at Lighthouse Park, a spoonful of green with a few benches shaded by young maple trees. Next to the water's edge were several marble seats, placed in memory of loved ones. I remember when this half-acre piece of land was a gravel and grass pullout, a place you could find spent condoms and empty beer cans. It reminded me how quickly the river changes, how a green stretch might soon be built up with condos or how once-active factories crumble to the ground.

In the middle of the river the squat, wooden Esopus Meadows Lighthouse tempted me out, but I wanted to save every bit of energy for our final three-and-a-half-mile push south to Esopus Island.

"I'm tired," I confessed.

"You know, you can drift," Emmet said.

Drift? I rested my paddle across the cockpit and leaned into the seat that cradled my body. Like a murmur, my boat continued south with the last of the ebb tide. It was an uncanny feeling, to move without effort, but I crossed my arms and let myself go, dipping my paddle only to adjust my course. Would it be possible to let the river take me where it wanted? If I floated in and out with the tides, where would that land me?

I'm told that a stick dropped in the water in Albany takes nine months to make it to the mouth of the river. Nine months, the time it takes to create a human life. Could the river birth me anew? Not on this trip. I could leave behind my final grades and the garden that needed weeding—I knew too well that they would be waiting for my return. But I could not paddle away from thoughts of my mother. In the rhythm and silence of paddling, my fears and sadness took shape.

I soon took up my paddle. I like leaving many aspects of life to chance, but this was too much. I needed to keep moving down the river. Movement gave me purpose, something to do when there was nothing I could do. I did not want to drift into my loss.

◊ ◊ ◊

To travel north to south on the Hudson is to travel toward civilization and density, both on shore and on the river. Traveling downstream was also the natural course as we united with the river's purpose of joining the sea. Traveling the other direction—south to north—is the course of exploration. In reading eighteenth-century travel narratives, I'm struck how everyone wanted something from the river. Peter Kalm, a Swedish naturalist working under Linnaeus, arrived in 1749 to gather seeds of herbs and trees for the Swedish Academy of Sciences. Richard Smith, journeying up the Hudson to survey a land grant in 1769, wanted what many did—to make money. In his narrative he notes the rich soil and fields of wheat and rye; he admires the sloops sailing north and south, thirty-one of them at that time, making eleven or twelve trips a year, and hauling 400 to 500 barrels of flour each. All this spelled cash. In 1776, Charles Carroll, who signed the Declaration of Independence, and became a United States Senator for Maryland, was part of a special commission sent north on the river to convince the Canadians to join the Americans in their efforts at liberation. Science, money, and politics moved people up and down this river.

How did I fit in with these narratives? I did not need to bring home seeds, money, or the hope of freedom. But I shared one element with these early travelers on the Hudson. As they worked north, they did not know what they would see or experience. To a large extent, neither did I as I moved south. The difference was that I could have known more, could have plotted our lunch spots and campsites. I was carrying with me a good guidebook, the *Hudson River Water Trail Guide.* It offered advice on where to put in and take out and mile-by-mile information on the sights on shore. But I hardly turned to it for assistance. Through my life, I have resisted planning trips, leaving much to chance. This is because I don't want to see what the guide tells me is supposed to be there; I want to see what I see, to have a direct relationship with the land and water.

Lung cancer comes with its own guidebook, full of chapters on early detection, treatment, clinical trials, care, and grieving. Some provide hope, but most share statistics that make it pretty clear that a five-foot-one, eighty-year-old French woman won't be in that slim percentage of survivors. I did not want to read that guidebook either.

Two days after we learned of the tumors in my mother's brain, I arrived home in State College, Pennsylvania, at the house I had grown up in. My tall father was crouched in the garden, beige work pants dirty, his turtleneck baggy on his solid frame. When he stood, he looked a little stooped. As I approached across the small lawn, he smiled and threw open his arms, his soft cheek resting on top of my head. We swayed back and forth, a soft hum rising from his throat; he didn't let go. I brushed away the tears before finding my mother making tea in the kitchen. I expected her to be changed, yet her short black hair framed the high cheekbones and strong eyes I loved. She held her chin high and gave a little skip of happiness when she saw me. My hands on her rounded back could feel her fragile ribs. For a brief moment I rested my cheek on the top of her head.

We had lobster for dinner, as if celebrating. They had kept their news to themselves, waiting to share it with their many close friends.

So this was the first chance they had had to speak about *what next* with someone else.

"I didn't want this for you," my father said, his big frame settling like a sigh into the wooden chair.

"I don't want anyone to feel sorry for me," she responded. "How many years did I have anyway? Six? Maybe seven?"

How could she be so fearless? I wondered. But our conversation didn't travel much further. Her words hung in the air. We strained toward cheerfulness and kindness.

My father and I offered to clean up after dinner.

"Go sit and read," I suggested.

"I want to play pounce," she said. Pounce was the card game we had played as a family, a version of solitaire, made manic with many hands shuffling, sorting, and piling cards. It required little skill except speed, which my mother did not have. Still, she was passionate about the game, her only card game. So she set up the cards while my father and I tidied the kitchen.

"You know what she told me?" my father asked as he figured out how to wedge a few more plates into the dishwasher. Laughter edged his voice. I could see that our somber mood was not going to last long. "I'll be breaking a lot of dishes, so be patient with me." We both laughed.

My mother broke dishes. Almost every plate in the house was chipped. A few years after their wedding my father wondered aloud what had happened to their wedding service. "I broke it," she said flatly. I also break and chip dishes. Is it possible that there is a gene coded for dish breaking? If so, I was happy to have it.

My father was patient and sweet and attentive in ways I had never seen before. Sitting over tea one afternoon, my mother told me about their trip to Hershey. They stayed in a nice motel, and in the morning, when she stepped out of the shower, he was there holding a towel to enfold and dry her. "He's never done that before," she said with a shrug and a half laugh.

He was not, however, so kind as to let her win at pounce. And neither was I. As we sat around the dining room table, my mother cursed in French while I told my father to stop breathing so heavily.

He claimed his cards were sticking and that he couldn't see for the glare of light. And then out of this chaos of complaints, the gloating cry of "Pounce!" would end one game. We would separate cards, count points, shuffle, and launch into the next round. And my mother lost, as surely and as cheerfully as she had her whole life.

◊ ◊ ◊

Emmet and I coasted onto Esopus Island, so wonderfully isolated. Without effort I unpacked, set up my four-season tent, and stretched out on my sleeping bag to rest for a moment. Emmet secured his hammock to a nearby tree and attached a tarp to keep the rain, which had chased us on and off all day, from drenching him. As my back sunk into the Therm-a-Rest I felt a gathering of physical aches.

"This is perfect," Emmet announced, cocooned in his sleeping bag in his hammock. His oar leaned against a tree while dry bags of clothes and food littered the ground. *Huck Finn,* I thought.

It wasn't yet time to sleep, so we set out to explore our island. We had barely entered the woods at the interior of the island when nesting Canada geese screeched, furious at our presence. A Canada goose is a big bird, not one I wanted to tangle with. We turned back, and settled on a nearby rock outcrop where someone had graffitied, *Cheryl, I love you.* I wondered who was so ambitious with paint and love to paddle out and mark these rocks. And, I was a little envious of Cheryl, whoever she is.

Later in the evening, I phoned my parents, standing on a rock on the north end of the island. They were on the line at the same time, my mother on the upstairs bedroom phone, while my father spoke from downstairs in the kitchen. There was little to report from their end, just another day with no appetite, with a visit to one in the army of doctors. And there was more chemotherapy.

I told them what spread before me: to the northeast, the serene-looking marina at Norrie Point, sailboats rocking in their slips, a fish—I claimed it was a striped bass—that leapt into the air, the stretch of the river in both directions open. I knew none of these things interested my mother, but I kept going.

"It's a big river," I said, "like the ocean."

"What are you going to eat for dinner?" my mother interrupted.

"Peanut butter."

"You should eat something better than that."

I laughed. She was right. Before hanging up, I said, "Courage ma petite maman."

Everyone I meet has a story of cancer. A grandmother, an uncle, a cousin, a best friend, a child. It is in every family, every life. Again and again I have heard of doctors who declared, She or he has six months to live. Then the person defied those odds, living on much longer. Or else died too soon. These stories were not my mother's story, so I did not listen closely.

My mother's doctors had not given us any time frame. They went through the motions as if my mother would live forever. I was grateful for their optimism yet angry they would not tell us what they no doubt knew. If I knew we had only three months, I would have chosen to spend every minute at her side, rubbing her neck that was always aching, holding her hand as we walked in front of our house admiring the columbine in bloom, listening to her talk with the hope she might tell me a story about her life I needed to know. If I had known we had only three months, I would not have been sitting on an island in the Hudson River.

◊ ◊ ◊

In the morning, the river appeared glassy, not a ripple disturbing the surface. We packed up, me a bit groggy without my morning coffee. Suddenly the wisdom of traveling light—without stove and pots and pans—was questionable.

We glided out, as serene as the water. For the first few miles, the river continued lazily, the land green and sloping to the water's edge. The train tracks on both shores move inland at this section, leaving the riverbank natural and quiet. All of this beauty contrasted with the gloomy sky that threatened more rain, and muted the color of the gray-brown water.

We stuck to the western shore. To the east was Hyde Park, though the town, as well as the home of Franklin Roosevelt, was not visible from the river. A few houses spotted the shoreline. By late morning, I realized that the idle current was not so idle; it was moving north, against us. The convergence of fatigue and lack of coffee hit me hard.

The river just north of Poughkeepsie squeezes in—this is the Lange Reach or Long Reach. Seen through tired eyes, that narrowness made it feel stingy, the sights on shore few. The lushness was monotone. I needed something to cheer me onward, a bit of graffiti or a crumbling factory. Not soon enough, we pulled up at the wooden dock at Mariner's-on-the Hudson in Highland.

The restaurant at the dock had not yet opened for business, but a nice waitress gave me a cup of lousy coffee that tasted perfect. I called John Lipscomb, the captain of the Riverkeeper boat, the *R. Ian Fletcher*. He would be able to tell me about the currents and tides.

John's mother and mine had been close friends, two French women who met in graduate school in Iowa City. After several summers spent together on Cape Cod I thought of John as a cousin, the kind you want to marry. He was slender and always tanned, with straight brown hair and a distinguished nose. In 1971 when he was eighteen, he and his father set out with a crew of friends to sail around the world. I was ten and found the stories that trickled home of Samoa or of Polynesian girls beyond romantic. For me, John smelled of water, whether ocean or river, and of freedom.

Now as adults our paths crossed on the Hudson River. We had had dinner a few times when he docked overnight in Kingston. His quick smile, often sardonic humor, and need to tease me had not changed. That he now wore glasses and his hair had thinned made him look wise; he was full of a seasoned knowledge about the river. The river I was coming to know is fully his home. He loves the river as one might love a child, with a protectiveness that bursts from time to time into outrage.

When I reached him by cell phone, he was out patrolling, taking water samples for an ongoing scientific study and checking on illegal discharges, just north of us. I could picture him in his low-lying boat, the small cabin where he slept through warm and cold nights while on patrol. All his samples and endless paperwork would be neat as can be. He would be wearing a white T-shirt, work pants, and a baseball cap.

"When will the current change?" I asked. One day out and I understood how essential it was to let the current work for us. On my day paddles I was fine fighting the current for an hour or two, but all day in a loaded boat was a different story.

It took John a long time to come up with an answer, and for a moment I thought he had hung up or that our call had been lost. Finally his voice emerged. "Two, two-thirty," he reported.

"This is more complicated than I thought," I said.

"It's all complicated, pal. How's your mom?" The way he said it made it sound like one sentence, and not a question.

"She's doing OK. She's amazing, never complains."

"I know about those tough French ladies." His mother had died two years before. At her funeral service my mother described lying on the beach with Roberte, who was pregnant with John. She dug a hole for her belly and nestled into the sand. It was as if he had grown with the ocean in his blood.

"Hang in there," John said.

"Thanks," I said, and folded my phone into my pocket.

◊ ◊ ◊

Emmet and I dozed as we waited for the current to change. Dan, an enthusiastic kayak guide appeared, waking us from our slumber. He wanted to know where we had come from and where we were heading. Dan had lots of information on where to cross, what currents to be aware of, and which towns we had to visit. Emmet took note of every landing and crossing and asked eager questions that showed we had little idea what we were moving into.

"My arms already hurt," I complained.

Out of the back of his van, Dan produced a first-aid kit. He handed me a few Advil as well as an ace bandage to wrap my arm. Next to the first-aid kit were stacks of fancy light paddles and life jackets. Dan was ready for anything on the river.

As we geared up, Dan looked at Emmet's canoe and reached for his oar. He handled it gingerly, as if turning over a relic.

"He made it himself," I bragged.

Dan nodded and gave me a crooked smile. As we loaded ourselves into our boats, Dan offered a few more suggestions on where to camp. Perhaps if he gave us enough information we would be safe. "These aren't in the guide, but they are perfectly legal."

"Are there trees at those locations?" Emmet asked.

Dan looked puzzled and shrugged his shoulders.

"I have a hammock," Emmet explained.

Dan shook his head. "You're killing me, kid."

As we paddled off, Emmet said, "I hope we meet lots of people like Dan."

There are a lot of people who love the Hudson, but not a lot of people like Dan who know her bends and eddies, and where it's good to camp. When I do meet someone on a dock or at a town landing our shared words are few: "Beautiful day" or "Doesn't get better than this." On this trip, we met no one else; the shores of the river were deserted. Then again, why would anyone be sitting next to the river in the rain? We were the nuts weaving about in the damp and cold.

South from Poughkeepsie, the river continues narrow and straight. Just out of reach of the roar of traffic on the Mid-Hudson Bridge, we traversed the river to sidle up next to the dramatic Trap Rock quarry at Clinton Point. Now owned by Tilcon, the quarry remains active with steel belts and rock-crushing machines visible for a mile-long stretch of the shoreline. The massive series of gray and beige towers and rugged steel conveyor belts loom over the river. This is just a slice of the 1,200 acres that the plant covers. Inland rests the deep hole from which since 1879 dolomitic limestone has been extracted by a series of companies, all working to provide rock for the foundations for New York State roads. By one estimate, there is another 200 years of rock in the ground. There are still several large active quarries along the river, but many have a buffer of trees and bushes between the river and the central plant operations. The scale of the Trap Rock quarry, though, is so spectacular it takes on its own somewhat monstrous beauty.

Late in the day, we arrived at Brockway, one of many former brick-yards in the valley, where the landing is pure brick, all covered in green algae. A vague sewage stink rose from the muck. We tried with no luck to find a place to set up tent and suspend hammock, as poison ivy looped in vines up the trees and littered the forest floor. We needed a little energy to keep moving, so after a handful of gorp, my favorite mixture of nuts and dried fruit studded with M&Ms, we pushed south, passing under the symmetrical, steel Newburgh-Beacon Bridge.

We needed to cross a minor bay between Beacon and Denning's Point, where we hoped to camp. It was not a broad stretch of water, but in the near dark it expanded, the land retreating as I supposedly advanced. I thought for a moment that I might not make it, that I would spend the rest of my life completing stroke after useless stroke in that desolate bay.

We paddled side by side as the sun vanished.

"I'm pooped," I said.

Emmet laughed, then launched into a story of where the expression came from. During stormy weather sailors stay alert, watching the rear of the boat for waves that might overtake the ship. If a wave swamps a ship from behind, it is pooped. Emmet rattled on with sailing expressions that have been loaded into our speech: "footloose and fancy free," "as the crow flies," "knowing the ropes," "pipe down," "three sheets to the wind."

Emmet's pleasure in nautical language was similar to my own at his age, though the language I learned was that of a climber. Standing around the local climbing shop when I was fifteen, I listened and imitated until I too was talking about bombproof belays, pounding in pins, and barndooring off a layback. I amassed gear so I could clip my biners and take a screamer off a hex, and I adored my stoppers and those new, miraculous inventions, Friends. It was that world that had seduced me as much as the climbing itself. I wondered what delights of language the kayaking world would bring me.

Despite all odds, we did land. We set up camp and tucked into a slab of bread slathered with peanut butter, which in such short time had lost all charm. Arms spent, we congratulated ourselves on the twenty-four miles covered. We sat in the dark, listening to the water lap onto shore.

"Does it look like the water comes this high?" I asked. My tent was wedged onto a narrow strip of land marked by smoothed rocks. We peered at the ground, looking for that mark of flotsam—sticks, plastic bottles, and water chestnut pods—left by the high tide. It did bisect my tent, but I didn't want to believe it. I was too tired to relocate.

"It might," Emmet said. "I guess we'll find out." He disappeared into his sleeping bag, one arm dangling over the edge of his hammock. "If the water rises, I'll feel it," he assured me.

Near midnight Emmet called out, "Susan, the water's at the edge of your tent."

I unzipped the tent door and peered into the semilit night. Sure enough, a small wavelet lapped up, lifting the nylon floor. The water retreated, then a faint wave scooched under my feet, rising to where my knees rested. I thrust my feet into dry bags, thinking that the easiest solution. I lay still, imagining my stillness might stop the rising tide. But the next wave teased its way toward my thighs.

"Want help?" Emmet asked.

Yes, I thought. "No, it's OK."

In three loads I transported everything to the top of a small hill, and there I slept, dry.

Too soon, I heard Emmet call through my tent wall, "The tide has turned, let's go."

A cheerless rain joined us as we passed Pollopel Island, which most people know as Bannerman's because of the crumbling castle on the island that bears his name. It is a visible marker on the river, something that those riding Metro-North or Amtrak to or from the city note from the train's window. The building, complete with turrets and long, spiraling staircase, is reminiscent of a medieval castle, and for this reason alone is intriguing. Trees grow from windows, and the place has a haunted feel.

Bannerman was a Scotsman, who died in 1918, ten years into building his castle. He lived there and ran a retail store and mail-order business that sold military surplus, including guns and uniforms, many from the Spanish-American War. I wonder how beautiful little

Pollopel Island would be without the massive collapsed building on it. On the other hand, it is good to remember the range of imaginative, wealthy, but perhaps a bit mad, men who have called this river home.

We approached Cold Spring, which has a lovely riverside park and floating docks. At ten, the café on Main Street was still serving the breakfast special. Eggs and bacon have rarely tasted as good. We spread out at the small table, writing in our journals. I recharged my phone and used the bathroom to brush my teeth and splash water on my face. I wrote to my mother, who loved nothing more than a postcard, written before or after a meal, that said nothing: "We're in Cold Spring, and just had eggs for breakfast." She had sent thousands of such postcards in her life, leaving a trail of her travels through France. I have a few hundred in a bulging folder, her scraggly handwriting describing the essentials of life and always ending with "Je t'embrasse"—I kiss you.

We walked to the grocery store to buy fruit, yogurt, apples, and, to my horror, more peanut butter. But we had settled on peanut butter as the universal food that needed no refrigeration. We stopped in at the local kayaking shop, where Emmet bought a double paddle. His enthusiasm for his wooden creation had wavered. I bought gloves and aqua socks to fend off the cold water, and two sponges, one for Emmet. We were both waterlogged.

"Where are you going?" the woman at the counter asked.

"New York. We started in Tivoli."

"Cool," she said. "Too bad we've had so much rain."

As we strolled through town I called home. My mother had three more chemo sessions left, but the poison had taken its toll; she was almost silent on the other end of the line.

"How is your trip?" my father asked.

I launched into river tales, emphasizing the heroics of our long days and our landings in the dark.

"You sound like you are eighteen again," my father said in his "My daughter is a lovable nut" voice.

Of course he did not want me to be eighteen. When I was that age, I jumped in a VW bug and drove to Colorado with my friend Neil. We slept in parking lots and rock climbed every day. When I look at my eighteen-year-old students I see how careless and young they are.

"Why did you let me go?" I once asked my father. He looked at me stunned. "There was no stopping you," he said, as if stating the obvious. "God, did I worry."

That had surprised me. I knew now that they worried, always in silence. But they had never tried to stop my adventures. Now, they were encouraging this makeshift trip down the Hudson. I knew it was a great distraction, something to talk about that did not involve doctors. If they knew I was throwing myself into the woods and onto rivers, then life was normal.

"Keep having fun," my father said.

"Courage, ma petite maman," I said before hanging up. "I'll see you in a few days."

◊ ◊ ◊

We left Cold Spring and rounded Magazine Point on Constitution Island, West Point flanking the western shoreline. We passed World's End, where the bottom of the river drops to 216 feet, which is the deepest point of the Hudson.

Before us, in glorious full sail, scooted the *Clearwater*, a replica of a Dutch sloop from the eighteenth and nineteenth centuries. The sloop is built for the winds and currents of the river. It has one mast with a large mainsail, and a low draft for the shallower waters of the river.

Emmet had worked on the *Clearwater* during the spring, teaching children about the boat and about the river. He let out a whoop of delight. While I shimmied toward shore, and onward to Garrison, he paddled straight for the ship, which surged north with the wind. Floating near shore, I turned to watch. Somehow Emmet had managed to hoist himself onboard. His canoe rocked behind the boat. I was convinced I'd see it flip over. *Well, there goes Emmet,* I thought.

I sat contemplating what was next. I looked back at the territory I'd just traveled through. This reach, known as the Highlands, is a dramatic landscape, the mountains towering over the water. This is different from my reach, where the Catskills sit back a bit, allowing space for the river to breathe. In the distance, Emmet's canoe no longer bobbed north but, rather, was heading toward me. Half an hour later he arrived, out of breath and grinning. "That was definitely the sketchiest thing I've done in a while," he said.

I smiled, sharing his glee.

The rain resumed as we hunkered down to pass through a wooded stretch of the river with few houses and no factories. We passed Arden Point, Mystery Point, and the row of renegade small houses at Manitou. We slipped under the intimate Bear Mountain Bridge—Bear Mountain to our right, Anthony's Nose to our left—before arriving in Peekskill. We shuttled to the western side of the river to stay clear of the Indian Point nuclear power plant, which dominates the eastern side. One-third of New York City's power comes from the plant. But nuclear power has always been controversial, and this plant has its particular issues. Indian Point sucks up 2.5 billion gallons of river water every day to cool the plant. This warmed water is then returned to the Hudson, altering the ecosystem. In addition, millions—some say billions—of fish are killed every year as eggs, larvae, and fish are sucked into the plant. The Indian Point license expires in 2013, and the calls to build expensive cooling towers or, better yet, shut the plant down are mounting.

By six in the evening we entered the three-and-a-half-mile-wide, shallow Haverstraw Bay, which yawns like the mouth of the ocean. When water splashed on my face I tasted salt on my lips for the first time; it was the ocean. It was still raining. I was cold, and hungry; my arms ached. We dragged onto Croton Point. Out of my exhaustion emerged a dull elation, the sign of a good adventure. I wandered, solitary, around the point, which is a landfill grassed over. Then I explored a small encampment with a swimming pool and cabins for summer vacationers, before settling into my nest for the night.

The next morning the rain was joined by a strong wind from the north. When we plunged into Croton Bay we were nearly upended. Traversing the bay was impossible, so we pointed north, into the wind. I kept glancing over to check on Emmet in his open canoe, loaded with several dry bags. I wasn't sure what I would do if he went over. My left arm was swollen, and every muscle was tender. Each stroke stretched my determination.

On the eastern shore, bulky Sing Sing prison stares out at the water, as it has since 1825. I imagined prisoners there, watching our folly as over the course of the next hour we made our way to shore. Later I learned the winds and conditions are so often vicious in the Croton Bay area commercial fisherman call it the Croton Triangle.

I do not remember the blur of the next few hours. The diligent rain that had kept us company the entire trip turned to a torrent. And a cold one at that. The weather, which was at first a burden, was now a hazard. We stuck as close to the rocky shoreline as possible, hunched over in our boats, waves jostling us about.

My vista shrank as my eyes trained on the small apron of water in front of my boat, anticipating the next wave that might knock me over. We pulled onto a sandy beach to pee, the waves hurtling me onto the shore. I stepped out of my boat, my legs limp.

"My sister lives in Tarrytown," Emmet said. "We could pull out there."

Emmet had mentioned his sister before, but I had not paid attention; stopping before Manhattan never was an option. Now it was. Tarrytown was just around the bend. We had a way out. Ending the trip just because I was cold, wet, and tired was cheating. Yet I leapt at the idea. If we pulled out a day early I could be in State College a day earlier.

The disappointment at not reaching the George Washington Bridge swelled and then vanished inside of me. A half hour later, at the Tarrytown marina, we clambered over slime-covered rocks that had a vague rotting smell, and hauled our boats onto the wooden dock. Like two forlorn children, we stood in the parking lot of the marina, waiting for Emmet's sister to retrieve us. I no longer tried to stay dry.

Safe in the Tarrytown apartment, I showered and then slipped into my driest clothes, the trip suddenly and surely over. Emmet unfolded his charts of the river, laying them out the length of the living room. We tracked our journey, and he tried to interest his sister in the wonder of what we'd done, journeying into many unknowns.

I had gotten what I imagined from this trip—the elation that comes from the basics of air and movement. I had gotten something more as well. The river offered, in all of those clouds and rain, real clarity about the force of tides and of currents. Physical lessons don't always translate to life lessons, but some do. There was no reason to fight the tides, and being drenched by the rain was senseless.

The river forces were bigger than me, just as the cancer was more forceful than all of us. We wouldn't stop fighting, of course, but we had to understand the magnitude of our foe. My physical suffering would not save my mother. The point now was to seek comfort, together.

◊ ◊ ◊

"We're done," I announced.

"Oh, I'm so relieved," my mother said, her voice clear over the phone line.

So am I, I thought. The ground moved beneath me, leaving me woozy. "I'll see you in two days," I said. Two days felt like an eternity.

"How marvelous," she said. Her voice sounded stronger. "I can't wait to see you."

5

HOME

To get to State College from Tivoli involves a drive south on the New York State Thruway, and then west on I-84 to cross the Delaware River into Pennsylvania. The mighty Delaware, my father called it, distinguishing it from what he called the limpid Susquehanna, which I crossed a few hours later. Every time I drive this route, I wish that the welcome sign to Pennsylvania elicited pride or a thrill, the rush of the traveler hurtling home. But dullness settles in as the journey unfolds. Near Scranton and Wilkes-Barre, those demon anthracite towns, the traffic inevitably bunches up. Then there is the stretch on I-80 where I become sleepy, and then impatient to be home. I know the shape of the land, the broad valleys and lumpy hills often sliced open to allow for the road to pass through. Loose rock threatens to fall. And yet the ordinariness of this route has its own beauty, and the simple repetition of driving it had made me comfortable. Perhaps familiarity fosters this ease. I've seen something similar in long marriages. Commitment entails stretches of boredom.

When I arrived home in State College I expected a place to be set at the wooden kitchen table for me, and my mother handing me fresh fruit or a yummy new cake bought at the farmer's market. Instead, she was curled up in bed. She turned when I touched her back. She smiled and sat up. Her cheekbones were more pronounced, her gray-blue eyes clear.

"You look wonderful," I said, as I hugged her.

She gave a half laugh, dismissing my words. Her short hair, which had stayed black until the past year, had thinned and was now white. This uncharacteristic disheveled look intrigued me.

"Let's see," I said, turning to the back of her head. There ran a narrow scar where the surgeon had cut, removing a golf ball–sized tumor. When he came out after hours of surgery he found my father, Becky, and me holding hands in the waiting room. "Tom Rogers, your wife is one tough lady." We tried to smile. This was something we knew. "That tumor had pushed out her skull." To give us a sense of what that meant, he knocked a fist against the wall. "She had to be in pain." But she had never complained. We knew something was wrong only because she had lost so much weight and because she had trouble seeing.

"Looks good," I said.

"But I want a few more turbans. And some hats," she said.

So we went shopping. After picking out head scarves and hats for herself, she had me try on a large, floppy red hat. As the cashier rang up our goods I was surprised at the price.

"I don't worry about money anymore," she said.

I smiled at her pleasure at buying just what she wanted.

I took her hand as we walked back to the car. She looked at me, her new beige hat riding low on her forehead.

"Il faut tenter de vivre," she said. It was a line she had recited so often I did not know where it came from. It was a family line, like "Round up the usual suspects" or "We must love one another or die," that sprinkled our lives. She often said it in the face of a minor setback, making us both laugh.

How now to make meaning of these words? There was no clear translation of that wonderful word *tenter*. You have to strive to live.

Living was an effort, required energy, striving. Or the translation could be, "You have to commit life"—the counter to commit suicide. That was more dramatic, the choice to live. I saw that she was carrying on, choosing life when she could so easily let go. I admired that she was embracing that imperative, whether the source was genetic or poetic. Her days, absorbed by medical treatments and doctors, often held little joy. It was hard not to ask, What was she living for? But she was striving, she was committed.

My father had learned to cook, or at least to get a meal on the table. It was odd to see him in the kitchen slicing vegetables and grating cheese. The kitchen was her world, a messy place out of which she produced delicious meals. On Sundays there was a roast chicken, and at the end of the month when money was tight she would make spaghetti carbonara. We ate together, my father telling stories, recounting the plot of a book he was reading, often getting up to retrieve the book and read us passages. The poems—there was the summer he memorized large sections of *Paradise Lost*—overwhelmed me, but when he read the opening of *Great Expectations*, Becky and I rushed to the table, anticipating more. There was his polar phase, in which we learned of Scott and Shackleton and their heroic journeys south across the ice. And there were lots of family stories. We learned about Rogers, Gist, and Fox families from Kentucky and that I was named after great-aunt Susan Fox, the one who did not get married. But my father did not leave out the French side. He had learned the intricate genealogy of Jacquie's family, the Monteguts—who wouldn't want to be descended from the Monteguts?—and the Vermeils, who went to California looking for gold. As a kid, I knew we were rich in food and family.

One night, the three of us, a bit more cheerful than usual, sat around the dining room table. My father spread his arms, reaching toward us both and asked, "So, where are we going to be buried?"

Silence.

"We should know, right?" he said.

She nodded.

I couldn't believe they hadn't discussed this before now. I took a sip of wine. I was the only one at the table drinking.

"Let's have half our ashes at the dunes, half in Estampes."

The dunes were the Indiana Dunes, where my father had grown up by Lake Michigan; Estampes, a subsistence-farming village in the southwest of France, was where my mother was born.

She nodded again.

◊ ◊ ◊

My father's meals were not very cohesive. Every night, he put out half a dozen dishes that he hoped would appeal to Jacquie; a salad that blended the snap of bitter endive, a sweet crunch of walnut, and a smooth wash from salty blue cheese became his favorite dish, because she was always delighted to see it. "Hey, you made a salad," she would comment. But she only ever had a few bites.

My father no longer told stories at the dinner table. He sat, breathing heavily, eating his share and hers. Though we tempted and cajoled, my mother could not eat. One evening she gagged at the table, and then rushed to the bathroom to throw up. Unable to show our love through food, as she had done so easily for us, we were at a loss.

We tried to play our family game of pounce, but the games were so tame and gentle they hardly resembled the rowdy rounds we had played just a few weeks earlier. In the afternoons and late into the night, I rubbed my mother's shoulders, which never stopped aching.

Every day my father took my mother on a walk. He would point out the white, blue, or purple columbine in bloom, as well as iris in various shades of purple, bushy peonies that flopped over in the rain, forget-me-nots, astilbe, a gorgeous deep purple clematis clambering over an arch. The flower turned itself inside out, exposing its delicate, pollen-dusted insides. And then his roses, which had names like Blanc Double de Coubert, a variety that is white and has an exquisite scent. "Smell this," he would insist several times a day.

Then they would stroll the alleyway behind the house. I spied them one afternoon, his arms hanging loose along his solid torso. At six foot four, he towered over her; she looked up, listening to him. He bent to kiss her forehead, then reached for her hand as they moved cautiously down the rough pavement. I stopped with the shock of tears. It wasn't that they looked so fragile; it was that I had so seldom seen them like that together. When we walked as a family, my father and Becky, who was a runner, set off at a clip. My mother and I meandered after, holding hands.

Walks, naps, and a regular parade of friends made up the sweet part of my mother's days. She still took interest in articles that her young French friend Sylviane clipped for her on what was happening in France, and became excited when our neighbor Sandy brought her delicious cheese crackers, even though she hardly ate any. Both women were more my age than my mother's. She could count on them to talk about what they had read in the *New Yorker*, an art exhibition opening in Paris, or the latest book they had read. She was bored with her aches and pains, and with people asking how her chemo was progressing.

One day my father and I spoke with a nurse who suggested a few things to make life easier—sippy cups, nutritional drinks, and a spongy bed pad. We rushed off to buy these things and more, so grateful for something to do.

As we returned with our bundles she asked, "Do you expect me to be sick a long time?"

I hesitated a moment, unsure what she was asking. "We want you to be comfortable while you are." Her question haunted me. Did she imagine she was going to get well, or was she asking if we thought she would die soon?

Did I imagine she was going to get well or that she was going to die soon? Both would have been my honest answer. Holding these two beliefs in mind was an impossible, excruciating balancing act.

We visited doctors almost every day. I could barely keep track of all the tests, and all the resulting medications. I made lists of the pills and set timers so we wouldn't forget midday doses. Still, it was often a blur. One day the doctors showed us the results of a recent CAT scan, and we all looked at them rather dumbly.

My mother's eyes were cloudy with confusion.

"So what does this mean?" I asked.

"It means that nothing has changed," the doctor said.

We all laughed in a nervous way.

I drove on the way home, the weight in the car heavy.

"This is such a drag for you," my father said from the back seat.

"No," I said quickly. "It would be a drag except that I love you, and not just because you are my parents. Becky and I were talking about this last night, how lucky we are to have parents we *like*."

I was trying to cheer him up, but from the back seat I could hear his halting breath as he wrestled with tears. After two weeks they both encouraged me to return to my life, to go home. But when I pulled out of the driveway, waving too energetically good-bye—would I see my mother again?—I wondered why I was leaving. What was I going back to? *My cats, my garden, my house, my life.* That meant writing and the river.

◊ ◊ ◊

To get into North Tivoli Bay from the river involves slipping under the railroad tracks. The passageway is about twenty feet wide and serves as a funnel for the water moving in and out of the bay with the tides. Squeezed into such a narrow space, the water drops and picks up speed. If the current is with me I coast through with ease. But if the current is against me, it can be a fight, the water sucking hard through the passage. If the tide is high I have to bend, embracing my boat, to get under the rusted steel girders. One time I lingered by the opening until a train announced its arrival, blowing its horn as it sped through Tivoli. I tucked under the bridge and waited. When the train arrived, I was flattened by the roar from above. This is not an experiment I would recommend; for days after I was edgy.

Since the tracks were laid in 1851, these steel rails have transformed the fortunes of this valley. But the trains also changed the ecology of the region, cutting off many bays from the main river. North Tivoli Bay became its own secluded paradise.

The incoming current swept me into the bay. There, it felt as if someone had flipped a switch, turning off the current and the wind of the river. Everything stilled, the texture of the air silken, the sounds of a different quality, crisper perhaps. The contrast between the calm of the tidal marsh and the noise of the river reminded me that the river is an arm of the ocean.

A vast, placid opening rimmed by reeds and cattails welcomed me. I stopped paddling to adjust to the calm and to shake the wind out of my ears. To the side, near the riprap that supports the train tracks, stood a great blue heron so still I was surprised when it came into focus. The bird, objecting to my presence, took flight, a graceful explosion into the air. Its enormous wings began a steady beat. I understood its flight; I too wanted to be alone.

North Tivoli Bay lies within my reach. It is the bay that I paddle to when I need to feel the calm that comes in a place well known, peaceful, isolated from the rush of the world. It is a home without walls that allows me to dream. On this day, I came hoping it would contain my fear and sadness.

The bay is approximately 370 acres, surrounded by over 1,400 acres of woods. It is filled with creatures—beaver and muskrat, and an enormous range of birds from the marsh wren to the American bittern—and with plants like the fire-red cardinal flower, marsh marigold, and pickerelweed with its purple spikes of flowers.

My initial perception of silence soon proved false. As I adjusted to the bay and its life, I heard a steady stream of bird songs and calls, dominated by the red-winged blackbird, its raspy *conk-la-deee* echoing through the reeds. It is an easy bird to spot, with its vibrant red wing patch on a stark black body. Most of the other birds in North Tivoli Bay hide, their voices rising from the grasses and cattails.

I first paid attention to birds, learning their names and who they are, when I lived in Arizona. There, it was hard to miss a bird like the vermilion flycatcher, so red in the dusky landscape. And there, in the dry canyons of the Southwest, I learned the song of the canyon wren, the descending notes ending in a slurpy kiss. On the East Coast, birds proved more elusive, shrouded in tree cover or bushes. I began by listening. The marsh wren never disappointed with its staccato, noisy trill. At the river side of the bays, tree swallows swoop and chatter; near the woods rise the flutelike tones of the wood thrush as well as the otherworldly, spinning call of the veery. Late one evening an American bittern let loose its distinctive gulp. It was for the least bittern, as well as the Virginia rail, common moorhen, and sora, that Tivoli Bays are a designated important bird area (though the moorhen has not been seen there in recent years). Most of these birds are secretive, but I hope some day to hear a sora. "You'll know when you hear it," a friend promises. "Hearing a sora is an event."

Despite my bird companions, the sense of being alone in the bay took hold. I've hiked, biked, backpacked, climbed, and traveled throughout the world alone. I eat most of my meals alone. I live alone. I've edited two books on women's solo adventures. To go alone is natural to me. In order to go alone, however, I cannot feel alone. The physical isolation cannot have an emotional twin. I need to know that someone back home cares about me, wants me to return whole. Over the years, various friends and lovers have cared, but at the center had been my parents. Feeling that part of my home base was unstable gave this small solo outing a new dimension.

I journey alone with a reasoned fear—I know the real dangers of what I do, and the fear keeps me attentive. Yet I was still learning the dangers of this water world, so my fears were muted by ignorance. The only time paddling North Bay did not feel vast and safe was in the fall when duck hunters arrived. Their wooden blinds stand like derelict shacks amidst the reeds. One fall day I spied Mallard ducks dabbling nearby. Intrigued by their beauty, their teal heads and rusty chests, I cautiously floated forward. When I was close enough to touch one I realized they were decoys. I spun in my seat, feeling like a fool. A camouflaged hunter shook his head, gun draped at his side. I smiled goofily and paddled on, adrenalin surging through my system. It wasn't the gun that scared me as much as my realization that the hunter had been watching me. I felt vulnerable, exposed. How long had he stood there, watching my wonder at his fake duck?

◊ ◊ ◊

I leaned into the back of my seat and admired the light that played through the wild rice, phragmites, and hardy cattails. Phragmites are not native to the bays, but I welcome them nonetheless, as I enjoy the sound of the luscious plumes as they swish in the breeze. Spatterdock, with its thick, green leaves, lounged on the surface toward the edges, its fat, yellow flowers coming into bloom.

Then, as I always do in the bay, I started scanning the waterline for snapping turtles. Snapping turtles have a bad reputation; they sport a nasty temperament and an ability to break fingers. And, because they have saggy skin, wartlike bumps, and mud-brown shells that often look slick with algal growth, they are often described as ugly. But there is something so prehistoric, so monstrous, in the fleshy, clawed feet and almost-flat carapace that I find the turtle fascinating, even beautiful. Because the snapping turtle is so much itself I am a bit in love with it.

"Here snapper, here turtle," I called. My voice vanished in the silvery water. But I knew that a turtle would emerge; there are hundreds in North Bay. Sometimes it is the triangular head snaking through the water that lets me know one is near. Sometimes I am startled by the almost-flat carapace floating beneath the surface near my paddle. One time I saw a snapper spread-eagle, as if doing a dead man's float.

Scientist Archie Carr describes the snapper as a "big, aggressive, ubiquitous, and succulent turtle." Succulent. Turtle soup has gone out of fashion but was once popular, threatening snapper populations. Esther Kiviat, in her lovely book on Tivoli Bays, recounts the story of a man who used to hunt for turtles by walking barefoot in the water. When he sensed a turtle under his foot, he hauled it up. The belief is that turtles don't snap in the water. I have little desire to test the truth of this bit of folk wisdom.

Though aggressive in later life, the early life of a turtle is pretty precarious. Beginning in May, a mother turtle hauls onto land and travels to the perfect spot to dig a hole in which to lay her eggs. How she figures this out appears mysterious as turtles on the march cross roads and fields. What she is looking for is a location that will offer the right amount of sun and warmth to incubate her eggs. She digs the nest with her hind legs, then lays about twenty to thirty eggs, which look like small Ping-Pong balls. The mother then leaves. Her eggs are an easy meal for a hungry raccoon.

One spring, on an evening walk, I came across five turtles digging their nests near the granite gravel that underlies the train tracks. By July all five nests had been raided, the shells scattered like pieces of torn white leather. If the eggs are not eaten by a hungry raccoon, and they reach maturity, babies emerge around August. They are perfect snacking size for any large bird or, in water, other turtles. If the turtle survives these hazardous early months and grows to an adult size—thirty pounds is average, but some grow much larger—it has no predator except man. And taking turtles for food ended in the 1970s once scientists measured the polychlorinated biphenyl (PCB) levels in turtle flesh.

PCBs are one of the river's biggest environmental problems. First manufactured in 1929, PCBs are used in electrical equipment, such as transformers and capacitors. Though PCBs were banned in 1979, the year I graduated from high school, they are still found all over our planet. On the Hudson, General Electric is the villain, as over a period of thirty years it dumped up to 1.3 million pounds of this toxic compound into the river.

PCBs lodge in the fatty tissues of animals, humans included, and do not break down. PCBs, according to the Environmental Protection Agency (EPA) "have been demonstrated to cause cancer." In 1975, GE was forced to stop using the river to dispose of its waste. Since then there have been long debates about who pays for the cleanup and what that cleanup should be. Some advocate for leaving the PCBs to rest, fearing that dredging would disturb the settled chemicals. Others insist that the toxins must be taken out of the river.

Animals that contain less than 2 parts per million (ppm) of PCBs are considered edible. A 1980 study shows that Hudson River turtles have an average of 2,000 ppm. The best part of this study is that the researchers—Ward Stone, Erik Kiviat, and Stanley Butkas—made turtle soup to test how those levels of PCBs from the flesh of turtles move through the food chain. They cite their recipe from the *Joy of Cooking*, which calls the turtle "short tempered." Further, the cookbook does "not recommend attempting to prepare live turtles in the domestic kitchen." I imagine these three scientists in lab coats, the smell of onions and garlic hanging over the pipettes in the corner as a pot of soup bubbles on the stove. Hudson River turtle soup holds 230 ppm of PCBs.

Did my mother ever make turtle soup? Where did her cancer come from?

My mother never smoked. This was the first question people asked me. Or, rather, it was the first thing I clarified: she didn't bring this on herself. A third of all lung cancer victims don't smoke, but, still, it's a marked cancer. Lung cancer generates less sympathy. Soon after her surgery, bandages still swathing her head, she told me a story about one cigarette she smoked in Lisbon in 1941, offered to her by a Portuguese soldier.

"I didn't want to leave France, you see," she said. "But there was so much fresh food in Portugal, and we had been living with so little." My mother was incapable of self-pity, so I filled this in with what I had been told before, how they had no sugar, and how scarce food was once her family left Paris for the southwest of France. "And the soldier was so handsome and tall." She let out a puff of a laugh, and I laughed too, agreeing that good food and beauty can change opinions and plans. As she smoked the handsome soldier's cigarette she decided that leaving for the United States was not such a bad thing after all. The rest of the story did not need to be told. Coming to the States meant meeting my father. It meant having my sister Becky and me. My mother never left any doubt: that was the best possible life.

◊ ◊ ◊

I stroked past a raft of water chestnut and pulled up a leaf, which looks like a green doily. Water chestnuts are everywhere in the river, and in the bay the plant has a sheltered area where it can flourish. Still, channels, like watery roads, remain open.

There is so much water chestnut it would be great if we could eat it. But this species is not edible and has no other uses, though some say that in Asia it is valued for medicinal and even magical properties. Water chestnut magic?

What we do know for certain is that once the water chestnut takes hold it covers the surface of the water like a thick green mat. It is hard for the sun to penetrate through that growth; the water below has reduced levels of dissolved oxygen. Plants and many animals, especially fish, do not thrive in these lower-oxygen environments.

But peering closely at one leaf, I see that it is a beautiful plant. The frilly edges of the small leaves are delicate, and the air-filled pods that keep the leaves afloat are ingenious. The long, thin roots of the water chestnut dangle through the water like a tangle of kite string, allowing the plant to rise and fall with the tides. Buds form on these plants, ready to pop into white flowers mid-July. It is hard to believe that this delicate-looking plant produces a black, pronged seedpod that has the menacing name Devil's Head.

Seeing the water chestnut as beautiful is heretical in the Hudson Valley. It is uninvited and has taken too much room. It arrived at Collins Lake, near Scotia in northern New York State, in 1884. From there it wandered down the Mohawk. In the 1930s it arrived in the Hudson, where it now clogs bays and shallow waters from Troy to Iona Island, just south of the Bear Mountain Bridge. It stops there, as the salinity of the water is too high; water chestnut favors fresh, slow-moving water. In the 1960s and 1970s the state tried to eradicate the water chestnut using the chemical 2,4-D, with little luck. In Asia, Africa, and Europe where the plant is native, it is contained by insects. Importing some of those insects would create other problems, no doubt. But that option is being investigated. An active hope of keeping it contained is chestnut pulls, using either a machine or human muscle.

Many plants and animals in the Hudson Valley are considered invasive. Phragmites, the zebra mussel (which also is not edible; it clings to boats and clogs intake pipes), mitten crab (again, not edible), purple loosestrife, and the mute swan are but a few. But given how humans move around the world, it makes sense that plants and animals would as well, making their homes wherever they can.

These plants and animals invite reflection on all of our movement. Though I have moved a lot, I admire and envy people who stay put—in houses, towns, in marriages. To remain in a place is, in my eyes, a virtue, each generation sinking in deeper, expanding the family home, and centralizing the family story.

My parents moved from Chicago to State College in 1961, the year I was born. They bought our house in 1967, paying it off at $25 a month. Their marriage lasted. Now, in this moment of illness, such stability, such relationship to place, made the heartache bearable. We had each other, and we had friends.

In thinking about my mother and the life she had led, I was forced to see the choices I had made in my life. I had roamed the world, and my solo life had felt like freedom. Now, her life settled in a place, a marriage, a house, looked like what mattered most. I did not want to indulge in regret, but, floating there in the bay, I felt about as safe as a baby turtle.

◊ ◊ ◊

In North Bay, channels wander, then dead-end in reeds and grasses. On this day I stuck to the main channel, which begins about thirty feet wide and then narrows, as it carried me in a meandering manner toward land. I scooped around a bend and passed a wooden dock. This is the other way to enter North Bay, by driving in on a carriage road and carrying a boat down steep wooden steps to the water. At low tide, the dock rests in the mud.

I continued past the dock where the water becomes clear as it rushes from its source, the Stony Creek (formerly the White Clay Kill; Kill is Dutch for "stream"). I could see fish swimming about, and an assortment of dumped tires. Soon, the water became too shallow to navigate, so I turned, gliding back toward the river. Ahead, a ripple indicated movement from below. A creature surged across the open waterway, then turned back, slapped the water, and vanished. A beaver.

The beaver was the river's first source of cash. Dutch traders bought pelts from the Native Americans and trapped, killing hundreds of thousands of the rodents. By 1840 the beaver was rare in New York State. From my paddles, I sensed that the beaver is doing well in North Tivoli Bay.

Then a V appeared in the water, a shimmer that told me something was swimming my way. There was my turtle. I stopped, waiting for him to approach. Five feet from my boat, the turtle somersaulted in the water, its white belly exposed. I made a wish, as if seeing that turtle might bring me luck.

But what could I wish for? That my mother might get well. That would be wasting a wish. I had to wish for something real, not a dream. That she might not suffer. That she might know how I loved her.

6

A LIFE IN A BOAT

It was hard, at first, to know what I was seeing, a sort of glittering explosion of color on the water, like one of those kaleidoscope tubes I looked into as a kid. The sun, rising behind me, made the colors of yellow, red, blue, and white shatter. Dizzy, I looked away. As the kayakers approached, their boats became distinct, separated, but not by much: over thirty boats, most sleek fiberglass or Kevlar with a few wooden boats wedged in, swarmed the Esopus, which runs out of Saugerties.

At the head of the pack was Dan, whom I had met on the river when I was paddling with Emmet. He greeted me cheerfully as he led this group of kayakers participating in the Great Hudson River Paddle on their journey from Albany to Manhattan. On this day, they would journey from Saugerties to Norrie Point. This was their fourth day on the river; some would make the whole journey; others like me were there just for the day, to catch some of the fun of this event—a sort of watery parade. But I also wanted to meet other kayakers.

I met people in kayaks on the river all the time. Many people buy plastic boats, as I first did, and throw them in the water on a beautiful day. I like that people want to be out, but these people in boats are not *kayakers*. I wanted to spend a day with kayakers, to know who these people are. Perhaps I was looking for more kin, more community.

Through my life, I had wedded myself to several communities: the ragtag group of climbers from the 1960s and '70s at the Gunks, the writers I met in Tucson, the farmers in my mother's village of Estampes, my good colleagues at Bard, and now the village of Tivoli. Some of these groups were more cohesive than others, and I needed them all in different ways. Did I also need a group of kayakers to give me more ballast in this world?

◊ ◊ ◊

The kayaks surrounded me, then spread out in a long line, north to south and facing east. From the south a guide announced that all was clear; from the north another guide echoed the same. Someone gave the call to move, and we did, flooding across the river. From inside the mass of twirling paddles I was pulled along by the movement, but was also a bit nervous about running into another kayak or slapping someone's paddle with my own. This was the first time I had crossed the river without swinging my gaze north then south to be sure I was clear of all boats. I liked that the mass of boats, each slim but together a formidable flotilla, protected me.

Once we were moving south, the boats spread out, a smear of color across the water. It was a beautiful sight. I slid toward the edges of the group, where there was more room. There, I tried to strike up conversation.

"Where are you from?" was a good place to begin.

"Nice boat" was another sure opener. And there were some interesting boats, especially the wooden ones, handcrafted and slim. Those kayakers used the thin, wooden Greenland paddles. One wore a T-shirt that read, "Paddle softly and carry a thin stick."

Conversations veered in a particular direction: good places to put a boat in the water. People told stories of lakes, rivers, bays, and oceans where they had paddled: the Bay of Fundy, the Maine Coastal Trail, San Juan Islands, the Outer Banks, Glacier Bay. I was happy on my river, but these names had a thrilling ring to them. As I listened I realized the names brought out a familiar wanderlust. When I was sixteen and heard of the Gunks, Eldorado, and Tuolomne I knew I had to go to those places. And then at those cliffs, certain climbs called to me: Foops, the Naked Edge, Golden Bars. The kayaking world held the same allure. One paddler grinned as she told me about Deception Pass, and a feature that sets up when it is flooding called the Room of Doom. "I almost lost my face," she said.

On the Hudson, I was often drawn out by the names of the river's features: Middle Ground Flats, Eve's Point, Ramshorn Marsh. What was it in a name that piqued my curiosity? I couldn't explain that, just as I couldn't explain why I did not feel compelled to launch out of Rensselaer, or why Hyde Park did not draw me in.

◊ ◊ ◊

The Great Hudson River Paddle, which had its first run in 2000, is a state initiative, part of the Hudson River Valley Greenway. To have kayakers paddling and camping along the river is but one means to get people to come back to the river, to see what was once a polluted waterway as a green (or greening) ribbon, a place to play and even to swim.

The paddle also promotes the idea of "the river that connects us, not divides us." I like the idea of this, and the larger sense of community that it engenders. But more and more I felt that the river did divide us and that division is not necessarily a bad thing. The river is a wide barrier, and that allowed towns to develop or rather keep their personalities. Within my reach, I realized that I essentially ignored the western shore—it was almost a mile away, after all. From time to time, I stopped at the Glasco landing, and I still regularly visited the Saugerties Lighthouse. But I never stayed long enough to know either place well. They had their own elaborate histories, town characters, and celebrations I would never be a part of.

We stopped on the end of Cruger Island in a scalloped cove where I had picnicked and rested many times before. I always find garbage at this site, left over from visitors who can walk out to the island at low tide. On the island, people build fires, cook out, and camp—despite all of the signs that warn against all of this. The kayakers clambered out of their boats to stretch legs and lower backs, then wandered into the woods to pee.

I wanted to tell someone stories of the island's past. Where we now splashed, poor boys from the city did as well, spending their summers at a camp on the island. If they followed the trail onto the island I could show them the brick remains of John Cruger's home. Or if we went east I could point out the eagle's nest, high in an oak tree. Instead, I sat quietly in my boat and watched as several paddlers took out bilge pumps and sprayed water high into the air, showering the group. And I was impressed by how some could roll their loaded kayaks, or lay them down in the water, sculling on the side to get wet but not go over. Everyone looked comfortable in their boats, expertly wielding their paddles.

I saw these kayakers do things I wanted to learn. In June, I had taken a daylong course with Atlantic Kayak Tours in Annsville, a large paddle center located near Indian Point. The young, articulate instructor talked about different strokes: forward, sweep, and sculling draw. He made me loosen my grip on the shaft of the paddle. "Keep your hand open, push with your palm," he explained. He helped me to visualize certain aspects of paddling. "Imagine an egg in front of you and you cannot break that egg." He gestured wide, creating a beach ball–sized egg in my imagination. I reached out, over that egg, extending my reach and bringing my torso to push as much as pull the blade through the water. He had us paddle as hard as we could, then glide, edging into our turns. I curved sweet turns in the placid bay. By the end of the day I no longer muscled my way forward, but rather experienced a new ease as I drew the paddle through the water. Never again would I end up with swollen forearms as I had when I paddled the river with Emmet.

I back paddled, then practiced a high and low brace, slapping my paddle against the surface of the water to keep from going over. And then over I went, grabbing the toggle of my spray skirt to slip out of the cockpit of the boat. I let my PFD lift me to the surface.

At first, jumping into the water there, with Indian Point nuclear power plant on the near horizon, felt a bit ominous. But I soon forgot the lurking menace of nuclear power as I focused on getting back into my boat. We practiced a range of rescues. The most basic, a T-rescue, is done by placing two kayaks at a T to each other to drain the capsized kayak of water. The two boats then run parallel. The swimmer mounts her boat, while the person afloat stabilizes it. We also learned what is known as the Hand of God rescue. Once over, you move your hand along the side of your boat, and another kayaker puts the nose of his boat where you can grab it and pull up. This requires strong lungs and enormous faith.

Most important for me, we learned to self-rescue. One method involves slipping what is called a paddle float over the end of one paddle blade and inflating it. I then used the paddle as ballast to stabilize my boat as I hauled out, dripping wet. It did not seem the most efficient way to reenter my kayak, but it worked.

At the end of the class the instructor pulled me aside. "It's clear you are the only person in this class who is going to continue paddling."

I smiled.

"You'll need these." He handed me a paddle float and a pump, to empty the boat of water for when I went over. "And this." He tossed me a tow rope, a small bag filled with a long rope. This attached to a belt that I could strap around my waist. If someone needed a tow, I could help. Or, I could toss the rope if I got into danger.

"And don't paddle alone," he advised. "Three is the minimum for safety."

I looked away. "Sure."

Later, alone on the river, I practiced falling out, and getting back in using a method taught to me by one of my students, Julia, who guided kayaks in the summertime. I mounted the boat like a horse then slid into the cockpit. "It's called the Cowboy," Julia explained with a grin. After this course I was not an expert paddler, but I was more capable, stronger. Added to this was the simple fact that day after day I was dropping forty-nine pounds of boat into the water. All of this had added up without my realizing it. I had come to feel comfortable in the soft black seat, my knees pushing up against the rests to keep a true line as I moved down the river.

◊ ◊ ◊

When we left Cruger and continued south, I dropped back a bit, to avoid the heavy traffic of boats. One of the guides, Mark, settled in next to me. He was of Native descent, with long hair tied back in a ponytail and large sunglasses dominating high cheekbones. His lean torso emerged as an extension of the kayak and led to polished shoulders. His boat was blue, with large patches fixed at the bow. There was nothing flashy or expert-looking about his boat. It looked used, lived in. As we used to say as kids, he looked like the real deal.

As we moved south, Mark offered pieces of his life story: he grew up in Westchester County, in a racially tense neighborhood. His story included years experimenting with drugs and alcohol, and trouble both with the law and in love. I believed him: he had that weathered "I've seen a lot of life" look to him, the raspy voice, an accent that is part southern, part street-smart. The story itself didn't surprise me— nothing much does—but something wasn't clicking.

"Hang on," I said. "How did you end up guiding kayaks?" In my question rests my understanding of the kayaking world as populated mostly by white, middle-class folks who live in rural areas. Kayaks originated as a tool for hunters. Close to the water, they could more easily spear fish. But modern kayakers are not out fishing; they are catching waves and having a good time. A kayak is expensive; storing a kayak takes room; getting a kayak into the water requires a car with a roof rack. It all assumes a certain level of wealth and of leisure time, and above all, a world where this sort of leisure makes sense. These people on this paddle had ten free days, after all, and a life that allowed for those days to be spent in a boat.

Mark's story did not explain why he was there, next to me in the Hudson River, but it went something like this: he got in a kayak on a lake in Tennessee, and after he took ten strokes into the water he looked back to shore and thought, *Good-bye backpack.*

I wanted to ask, Where did the backpack come from, and the kayak, who did it belong to? Why was he in Tennessee? But I decided to accept that he saw his life resting on a moment of revelation, one that led from those ten paddle strokes to guiding in the Bay of Fundy and back to the Hudson River. Those ten strokes led to a life in a boat. For all of the details that were left out, for all that was not explained, I understood his story. Or rather, it made sense to me. He was handed something—a boat—and he had made it his life. Chance and then will. I was handed the Hudson River when I moved to Tivoli. I did not choose the river, but I saw that I was lucky to have the Hudson to play on, to explore, to turn to for comfort. And now with effort and love I was making it my home.

7

THE LOST DUNES
OF CHILDHOOD

The Indiana Dunes shift with each season, the sand mounding up, then pouring down to the waters of Lake Michigan. The lake shifts too. Most days it is glassy calm, but sometimes waves whipped into life by wind crest onto shore. Or at least this is what I remember. My grandparents had a house perched above the dunes, with tempting views of the lake. But the house was sold in 1973, one of those family mistakes that lingers as regret. What remains are my memories of long days of sun, of sandy sandwiches, of energetic and often competitive games of croquet, and of my mother sunbathing as she did her whole life, pulling the straps of her one-piece bathing suit down so that she'd have golden brown shoulders.

My grandfather directed chemical research at Standard Oil, drove spacious American cars, and, with my grandmother, played bridge and golfed at the country club on the weekend. They were puzzled, no doubt, that they, two chemists, produced a son who was a writer, who cared little about money and a lot about books. And, the story goes, they were a bit dismayed that he had married a French woman who didn't bake and couldn't round out a foursome for a game of bridge.

At my grandparents' house I was in heaven. We ate popsicles that were in endless supply in the freezer, and we played games—everything from billiards on a pool table in the basement to flashlight tag in the dunes. Becky and I got up before dawn and plunked ourselves on the wall-to-wall carpeting just feet in front of the television to watch re-runs of Bugs Bunny cartoons and Captain Kangaroo. At home we did not have a TV. The house at the dunes smelled of cookies, and the basement of lawn-mower oil and cut grass.

But the best part was that there was always someone to play with. At home in State College I was often left to entertain myself while Becky disappeared with a book. Books did not interest me then. So I wandered next door to find Mrs. Stevenson, our neighbor, and the sort of mother who organized kids to bake muffins and whose dining room table was littered with dull scissors, markers, and colored paper.

At age four, I asked my mother, "Why aren't you a playful mother, like Mrs. Stevenson?" My mother thought this made for a funny story—the first bite of criticism from a child who adored her—and so she told it over and over. At the dunes, though, she was playful, taking us to the beach, where there was enough sand to keep me busy for a lifetime. And in his boyhood home, my father transformed from the writer who needed silence (the only rule growing up was "Be quiet, your father is writing") to the man, or maybe the boy—was he Tommy once again?—who bodysurfed when the lake became turbulent, who chased us for hours in games of cut the pie, who floated on his back in the calm lake, and stuck his big toe out of the water daring us to catch it. He was a cork, performing stunts in the water that made Becky and me squeal with delight. In the short man's backstroke, his long frame would miraculously fold in half as he slapped his way about, using his big feet as paddles. In the one-finger sidestroke, using just an index finger for propulsion, he would glide through the water. We tried to imitate these ingenious strokes only to sink into the clear water.

The highlight every year at the dunes was camping out. Once or twice in a summer we'd gather together our cotton sleeping bags (an olive color on the outside with scenes of dogs and hunting lining the inside), bags of chips, marshmallows, and sodas, and then head to the blowout to camp. The blowout was what we called the dunes in front of the house. A mountain of sand stood in the middle, flowing down to an open basin on one side and a swath of sand ringed by scrub oak and rhododendron on the other.

A few of the Kollar kids, who lived across the blowout, would join us in our campouts. They would bring a large cooler, adding to our soda supply.

We didn't sleep, of course. We played hours of flashlight tag or capture the flag, taking over vast stretches of smooth sand, and racing up and over high hills. Our calves stung with the effort. Later, exhausted but unwilling to sleep, we would dig a big pit and gather wood for a fire. Sitting around the blaze, we roasted marshmallows and ate the toasted, often burnt, sugar until we were queasy. And then we would set about terrifying ourselves.

A lot of time was spent speculating about the boys from down the beach who might come and raid us. We had heard about raids—how they took coolers (what could be worse?!) and smashed them, running off with the loot of sodas and snacks. That teenagers were not interested in stealing soda from children never occurred to us—those sodas and snacks were precious. So whenever the lights of a lone car traveled down the narrow road that ringed the blowout we would shower the flames with sand and lie still, bodies pressed against the ground, hoping that our camp would go unnoticed. I remember the texture of the fine sand against my cheek, and the sense I had that I could feel the heat from the day evaporating as I held my breath, waiting for the car to pass.

If these imagined raids weren't enough to fuel our fears, we called upon spirits to keep our nerves on edge. We held levitations and séances. Once Becky called on the spirit of George Washington. "If you are with us, have a dog bark three times," she asked solemnly. The neighbor's dog set to howling. Paralyzed, we stared into the dark, wondering where you hide when a spirit is about.

One night stands out. A storm was threatening, a hot electric storm of midsummer. Still, Becky and I, along with our cousin Andrew, headed out to the dunes, deciding that if it did rain we'd drag

ourselves home. We settled into a hollow at the base of the large sand
hill, built our fire, and thrilled that the storm added an extra element of excitement. We scared ourselves silly—could we be struck by
lightning and killed? And then the storm landed with a fury, racing
in from the lake. A bolt of lightning, and then another, pierced the
sky. And there at the top of the big hill, illuminated in those dashes
of light, was a ghost—unmistakable, white and tall. For an extended
moment the lightning lit the ghost from behind as it waved its arms,
menacing even at a distance. And then in the crackling dark we saw it
move back over the hill, out of our sight. Andrew sprung into action,
chasing the ghost.

I called to him, "No! Don't go!" Couldn't he see he was running
toward doom? I sped for cover in the woods.

An hour later I was found, crouched in the woods, well hidden.
Andrew, wiser at twelve than my ten, could tell the difference between
a ghost and my father covered in a sheet.

◊ ◊ ◊

My parents were bookish, generous, funny, sometimes playful people.
My father taught creative writing at Penn State and wrote four novels,
many essays, and a few short stories. His third novel, *At the Shores*, is set
in the Indiana Dunes. My mother gave up her job as a professor of
French literature to tend to my sister and me, but she was always busy
teaching French to children or adults or working on translations of
authors ranging from Alexander Dumas to Philip Roth.

We never had much money, but we had time—those long sum-
mers, the gift of the academic life, as well as sabbatical years that threw
us together in Paris in 1970 and in Estampes in 1978. My mother
had an army of friends, many with nice homes on Cape Cod or in the
Dordogne Valley, where we were welcome.

My father was a master storyteller, so that all of my school friends
wanted to come for dinner, for the good food and for the entertain-
ment. My parents' friends and colleagues stopped by after teaching for
a drink—my father's martinis were legendary in an era when a good
martini mattered—or for dinner, prepared so easily. There was talk

of books and politics. Sitting in the living room, in the company of those adults, I learned to think, and came to understand the riotous pleasure of ideas.

Yet it was also because of those days at the dunes with my parents that I've wanted to be outdoors. I have slept with my back to the ground from Alaska to the Antarctic. And one thing holds true: camping out is not about a good night's sleep. It is about walking into the dark and lying down, feeling both safe and scared. It was there in the dunes, in the sleepless early morning of my youth, that fear and adventure forever twinned.

Every so often, I smell, see, or taste something that reminds me of the dunes, and those days come back to me. Memories so lush and deep of a time when I was certain my small happy family was perfect, that life itself was perfect. The Indiana Dunes are my "lost woods of childhood."

This phrase comes from the nature writer Edwin Way Teale, who, after trying to find woods he had visited as a child, gives up. "At any rate, I never saw the ancient trees of that old woodland a second time. The Lost Woods of childhood remained lost forever. In talking to others, I have come to believe that most of us have had some such experience—that some lonely spot, some private nook, some glen or streamside-scene impressed us so deeply that even today its memory recalls the mood of a lost enchantment." I have never returned to the dunes, but I've often gone in search of places that remind me of those days of enchantment. If I find a landscape that echoes the feel or beauty of my childhood summers I sense an immediate affection for that spot. I've had this feeling many times before, but never on the Hudson.

Everything about the Hudson—the smells and texture of the land, the river and its culture—was initially foreign to me. There were no kayaks in my childhood. Because the river is outside of my experience, I do not kayak sniffing for places that resonate with the familiar. I don't round a bend imagining I'll be home. On the water, I have a blank page on which to find new woods, on which to create my own stories. On the river, I am like that child running down the sand dunes, looking forward to the next game of capture the flag or cut the pie.

8

THE SPEED OF WIND
AND WATER

It was an unbearably hot late July day, the sort of day that demands a nap. After that nap, I expected to feel renewed. But I was still cranky from the heat's constriction. I needed to move, and vacillated between walking or heading to the river with my boat. Hoisting my boat onto the roof of the car, strapping it down, making sure I had all of my gear, felt complicated, too complicated; heat makes the smallest gestures enormous. I decided on the walk.

I slipped out of the house, not bothering to lock the door. From each house down Feroe Avenue a hum emerged from a window as an air conditioner worked hard to make life indoors bearable. In the distance I could hear the bells of St. Sylvia's Catholic Church beginning their evening songs—Christmas hymns, oddly, even in the middle of summer.

The houses along Feroe, built around 1900, mirror each other: two-story boxes with front porches and narrow driveways. There are no frills, no garages or front yards, as all of the houses sit hard beside the one-way alley that calls itself an avenue. It used to be that one extended family—cousins, aunts, and uncles—lived in all of these houses. My neighbors, brother and sister Eddy and Marilyn, were a part of this family. "My grandparents had eighteen kids. My grandfather owned all the houses on this street. It was great," Eddy told me with a laugh.

"Eighteen? Eddy, you'd have to stack people on top of each other to sleep eighteen in one of these houses."

"I know," he said, shaking his head.

As I stepped out the front door, I hoped to see my neighbors, Ann Moore and Diane Lown, out on their back stoop smoking a cigarette. Ann had raised her family in the house, and now with her husband passed away and children grown—she has great-grandchildren—she shares it with her friend Diane. We discuss weather and health and the status of our gardens. And sometimes, they give me a snapshot of Tivoli from the past. There used to be a general store with a soda fountain on Broadway, and a meat market in town as well. Ann worked at the Confectionary, known to locals as the candy store, scooping ice cream. "I made the best egg creams," she told me with a smile. "You had to know what you were doing to get the froth on top." Ann now makes the best spaghetti sauce. On those days when she has been cooking, blending in the meatballs and sausage, I'll find a large portion in a Cool Whip container in my fridge.

Both Ann and Diane were inside, so I moved down narrow Feroe. It pleases me that in the early nineteenth century, Jacob Feroe was one of Tivoli's most enterprising businessmen. Feroe began his career as a schoolteacher in Saugerties and later taught in Tivoli (the Tivoli schoolhouse is now rented as apartments). Feroe also ran a fruit farm, a barrel factory, and a gristmill. The man was prodigious.

I turned right onto Broadway and passed a few second-generation Volvos with Bard College stickers on the rear window. Above those Bard College stickers are the emblems from an older sibling's college years: Hampshire, Reed, Oberlin. In one car, a heap of laundry rested in the backseat, likely either coming or going to the Lost Sock Launderette on the corner. The long brick building I walked along on the south side of Broadway was once a ladies' undergarment factory, which closed in 1970. Now, the second story has been redone into spacious apartments.

Left onto North Road. There, Queen Anne–style houses painted pink, white, and yellow are set back, framed by lawns and lush trees—locust, Japanese maple, tulip. A little ways down is the Trinity Episcopal Church, which someone has made into a private residence. A stone pathway, lined with small maple trees, leads from the sidewalk to the church-house. An obelisk in memory of those who died in the Civil War stands near the sidewalk. The owners of this former church also bought the defunct Methodist Church, with its slate spire, in the middle of town. For a while, they ran a deli out of the Methodist Church.

Further down is the white house of my friends Lisa Sanditz and Tim Davis, with the six-foot-tall statues of their cats on the front porch. The cats are made of wood covered with chicken wire then papier-mâchéd with broadsheets of the *New York Times*. They are painted in house paint, white and gray, with pink tongues. When I walk by I can hear Tim on the guitar, or see the lights on in Lisa's studio over the garage. Together they have organized an annual edible sculpture party, which draws in hundreds of people with inventive creations. One year a food-artist baked a Bo Derek cake, another a Yellow Submarine. Two sisters replicated the small wooden dock that someone had recently constructed at the Tivoli landing. They used pita bread, which looked as unstable as the dock itself, with the river made of guacamole. The color of guacamole, a bit brown from sitting in the sun, was troublingly close to the color of the actual river. The edible sculpture party lines up with a series of townwide events that bring us together. In the fall is Tivoli street painting day, when Broadway is closed off, and children and adults take chalk to the streets. In the summer is Tivoli yard sale day, when everyone empties out their wet basements and sells their goods. And then there is the annual pie contest initiated by Mikee the baker. What this all means is that I know—at least by sight—most of the 1,200 residents of Tivoli. I know the mayor and care about village issues, especially the decades-old riverside park proposal. If we build a park, we would have to build a pass over the train tracks. A park would be lovely, but my response to this idea is utterly selfish: I fret about how I'll get my boat in the water.

◊ ◊ ◊

On my daily walks, I enjoy watching the progression of flowers through the season and note when someone has repainted a fence, or a tree has collapsed due to an abrupt wind. Of all the streets of Tivoli, North Road is the finest. But Queen Anne architecture is by nature eccentric, and its intended asymmetry is taken to heart by many of the homes, which come off looking unbalanced. There is no consistency in the inconsistency. And wedged in there are two brooding houses, where I have never seen light or life. One homeowner imagines she lives in the deep country with her lot that has two horses standing placid in a mucky pen. In front of the garage is a clutter of stuff destined for the town dump. Out front a sign reads Good Cluckin Eggs; the chickens wander into the road, stopping traffic.

The houses vanish as the road dips downhill toward the Stony Creek, which I can hear off to my right as it surges after a strong rain. A house that was in ruins when I arrived in Tivoli stands shiny with not just new paint but a new roof, an addition, and a string of weeping willows by the white fence next to the road. The two men who fixed up this house also took the Morey, a local bar also known as Bayly's, in the middle of the village and made it into a first-rate restaurant and hotel they named Madalin. Their horses loll in the grassy field behind the house and stand in the shade in a small enclosure that has the same peaked roof as the house.

I used to think that walking and kayaking were similar—the one using legs, and the other torso and arms—each providing equal opportunity to meditate. But walking is not kayaking, it is not even close. Being on the water does magical things—purifies and heals, washes and cools, enlivens and frightens. This walk on hard, black asphalt made me hotter, as even at seven in the evening the heat from the tarmac radiated up my calves. As I walked I thought, *I made the wrong choice; I should have gone paddling.* Only paddling would have soothed me after such a day contained indoors.

Sengstack Lane curves west, braced by a horse farm to the north. Purple loosestrife, which puts out a three-foot magenta-colored shaft of flowers, ridged the road. The horizon opened, the sky rising higher, and above the trees in the distance swelled the hump of Roundtop. Catching this glimpse of the Catskills gave me an even greater urge to paddle, to work my way toward those mountains in the distance.

My cell phone rang.

"I'm thinking of going out." I recognized my friend Carol Lewis's voice.

"That would put us on the river around 7:30," I said, a hint of warning in my voice. I had been on the river at night, but it still seemed forbidden. I took the leap: "I'll meet you at the landing at 7:20."

◊ ◊ ◊

I had met Carol one evening a year before at the Tivoli landing. It was dusk when her boyfriend, Michael, pulled onto shore. He stood there, arms crossed, and looked into the distance. The sun had set, the air cold and the water colder.

"Are you waiting for someone?" I asked.

"Yes," he said, the slightest concern in his voice. "She likes to stop and look at things."

In the dark? I wondered. I looked north with him into an empty river.

"She'll show up," he said.

I left him gazing into the shadows of the night. By the time I had walked home I had started to worry about this person I did not know. So I drove back down to the river, where I found the two of them watching the river from their car, Carol perfectly safe. I couldn't tell if Carol was a bit crazy or just wonderfully adventurous, but I was intrigued to find out. "If you want to paddle, call me," I said and gave her my phone number.

I did not expect Carol to call, but she did, inviting me to join her on her frequent evening paddles. For her devotion and time, this was her reach as much as it was mine. I often wondered how many others called this stretch of river their own.

On our outings, I enjoyed Carol's directness and humor. I learned that she had one son, was raised Catholic, and that she had met Michael online. "I never thought I could love a lawyer," she mused. She was a mixture of drifter and danger-seeker; I liked being on the water with her.

◊ ◊ ◊

I raced through the final mile of my walk, through the thick woods dominated by tall oak and maple trees on Woods Road, south with the development on the eastern side of the road, the brick Episcopal Church on the west. Back on Broadway, I ran past the three-story brick Watts de Peyster building that was once the fireman's hall and now houses the village offices and our busy, warm library. I loaded my boat onto my car with gusto and drove to the waterfront. Carol arrived at the Tivoli landing shortly after me. We helped each other to place boats in the water.

"Let's head north," I said. That would put us against the current.

The sun lingered over the Catskills, creating an orange-pink glow. This sunset was a cousin to those painted by Frederic Church over a hundred years ago. Realizing that Church's work was more realistic than not made me warm to his vision. The near-garish colors framed the mountains, and the water echoed the display by glimmering black. It was beautiful, and, I had to admit, so were Church's paintings.

We stroked toward the middle of the river. Most of the motorboats had already docked after a day on the river, so we had the water to ourselves. We could see for a long distance both north and south sheer to the Kingston Bridge. As we moved north, our conversation mimicked the currents of the river, meandering from one subject to the next, then returning to where we began. Neither of us was concerned with our lack of conclusions. We discussed the imminent return of Carol's boyfriend ("Six weeks is a long time," she said), the works of John Steinbeck and Hal Borland, and the life of the spirit. But when you kayak the subject so often turns to weather: fog, wind, rain, and lightning. Weather is the great common conversation. It is how all good adventure stories on the water begin.

"Once I was out with Charlie," Carol began. Charlie was a local who launched his kayak out of Glasco. Sometimes he would paddle up next to me and tell me where he had been, what he had seen on the river. I had a sense he knew the river well. "We were heading toward Saugerties on the western shore." Carol laughed, anticipating the next sequence of her story. "The fog was so thick I couldn't see him ahead of me; we had to talk the whole time. We couldn't figure out where we were, and then we saw lights on shore." She hesitated a long moment. "They were the lights in Tivoli."

I made a noise like a laugh but was shaken with disbelief, that the fog had disoriented them in such a fantastic manner—they were heading south on the eastern shore when they thought they were paddling north on the western shore. "You crossed the river?" I asked.

Carol laughed, a half giggle. She too knew her mistakes made for good stories.

◊ ◊ ◊

When I think of places controlled by weather I think of the heat of the desert Southwest, the cold of the poles. The Hudson River Valley is a mild place in comparison. Still, our weather has meaning.

I had a student who grew up in San Francisco. What drew her to Bard was that her grandmother lived in the Hudson Valley; it was the place of summer vacations, and of hot sunny days. She couldn't understand why when she called her grandmother in the fall and winter the conversation inevitably turned to weather. But after she had staggered through her first year she saw how the snow, sleet, and rain controlled her health and her moods, or determined whether she missed class because it was just too awful to go out. The endless cold gray of March, when the cloud cover hardly lifted, had nearly done her in that year.

And yet it is easy to excuse those awful March days because the rest of the year is so often lovely. The spring woods are filled with warblers, and the explosion of green growth gives hope new meaning. Falls are exquisite; hoards of leaf peepers drive up from Manhattan to taste the crisp air, to buy apples, and to glory in the orange, yellow, and red colors of the trees.

When Henry Hudson sailed up the river in 1609 his right-hand man, Robert Juet, kept good stock of the weather. It's the first thing he notes in his daily log, and out of the twenty-three days in September and October that they spend on the river, twenty are reported to be "faire" or "very faire." Fair: *free of clouds or storm; clear and sunny.* The *Half Moon* experienced a day where it was misty until clear, and two days where a stiff gale kept them at anchor, or, as Juet writes, "we rode still."

All we have of Hudson's trip up the river is Juet's journal, as Hudson's own journals, logbooks, and charts were sent to Holland on his return, and little remains of them. They were destroyed, sold, or lost. Hudson was, as Douglas Hunter writes in his engaging history of the 1609 voyage, a "self-interested explorer." His trip up the Hudson violated his contract with the Dutch East India Company, which had tasked him with finding a northeast passage. America is surely west of the Netherlands. I wonder if Hudson's journals revealed his motives (or his greed) and for this reason conveniently vanished. In any rate, what we have are the words of Juet, one of four Englishmen on board, for a glimpse into this famous expedition, the first observations of the river made by European eyes.

When I read Juet's journal, I want in on this voyage, to feel the miracle of seeing this land in such a pure state. We see the waters teeming with fish: "They tooke four or five and twentie Mullets, Breames, Bases, and Barbils," he writes on the 27th of September 1609. He also writes of pulling salmon out of the river, a fish that Robert Boyle claims never swam in the Hudson. Juet also notes the "goodly Oakes and Wal-nut trees, and Chestnut trees, Ewe trees, and trees of sweet wood in great abundance, and great store of Slate for houses and other good stones." The natural world of 1609 is wonderfully rich.

Of the land just south of my reach, Juet writes, "This is a very pleasant place to build a Towne on." It was beautiful. It *is* beautiful.

But Juet does not give us many visuals. What we have in detail is the depth of the water—they run aground a few times and have to wait for high tide, and often they encounter "soft Ozie ground." And, he makes note of the wind.

◊ ◊ ◊

One summer when Becky was seven and I was five, my father took us to a place he called the windy spot, in the south of France. At the top of a red sandstone cliff stood a metal tower facing the wind that sailed in off the Mediterranean. We raced up the tower and threw ourselves into the wind, which tangled my shoulder-length hair. We might have been carried off except that my father crouched behind us, one arm around each of his daughters, and held us against his body while we laughed in fear and glee. Every day we clamored to return to that spot.

As an adult I've been drawn to places like Argentina and the Antarctic, where wind rules the land. Caring about wind, I have become intimate with the Beaufort scale of wind. Francis Beaufort established this scale in the nineteenth century, the golden age of observation, when scientific men were studying the natural world in order to make sense of it, arrange it, and make it neat. These classifications served exploration, travel, industry, and agriculture. Beaufort's classification was complicated because what he wanted to make consistent and universal was something invisible. Invisible because you cannot see wind, you cannot hold wind. You can see only the effects of wind.

The Beaufort scale offers a way to measure the wind from 1 to 12 (12 is a hurricane; hurricanes are further divided into categories 1–4). This can be done using an anemometer, a simple device that I carry in my pocket. But even without the device, I can tell if a wind is too much for me. If the wind is moving leaves and branches near my house on Feroe, it will be blowing too hard on the river.

We live in a world of scales to measure the invisible: "On a scale of one to ten, your pain is what?" the doctor asks. Only my mother could tell us when the pain had become too much. "On a scale of one

to ten, how lonely are you? How sad are you?" Only I could tell that
my numbers on these scales were too high.

◊ ◊ ◊

Beaufort's is not a simple scale. Each number has a corresponding name—
calm or fresh breeze or moderate gale—as well as a description of what
the wind does. Level 3, a gentle breeze: "Leaves and small twigs in constant
motion; wind extends light flag." Or level 9, a strong gale: "Slight struc-
tural damage occurs; chimney pots and slates removed." Or, my favorite,
level 5, a fresh breeze: "Small trees in leaf begin to sway; crested wavelets
form on inland waters." As Scott Huler notes in his marvelous book on
Beaufort, this is in iambic pentameter. Poetry to describe the wind.

With Beaufort's scale, I could read Robert Juet's unadorned journal
in a new light. Juet's "stiff gale" that kept them from sailing one day
must correspond to Beaufort's "fresh gale," a level 8 wind, 39–46 mph.
"Breaks twigs off trees; generally impedes progress." Beaufort's scale
makes what these men did more vivid, more real. I can see the *Half
Moon* rocking in the waves of a stiff gale. I know how the winds on the
Hudson careen out of the north, then unexpectedly appear from the
west. If these strong winds push against the tide the waves swell, with
cresting whitecaps. And strong winds knock trees and branches into
the river. Boaters call these floating logs widow-makers for a reason.
Of course the *Half Moon* "rode still" during these stiff winds. Never
would I venture onto the river in such weather.

Beaufort's goal in creating his scale was to make our understanding of wind universal. A sailor coming from the West Indies could
describe the winds there, and a captain who knew the north seas would
know what winds he might encounter. That I am translating the wind
of almost 400 years ago to the present means that Beaufort's dream is
extended: the wind is also timeless. Juet's wind could blow today.

◊ ◊ ◊

The sun began to sink, and Carol and I paddled as if on a long, watery treadmill. To the east rested Rose Hill, elegant, serene, and never

vanishing from sight. The going was slow, with the current against us. The speed of water is, like wind, invisible until you see what it does, what it moves. I watch the water for swirling patterns that indicate a shift in current. Still, currents do take me by surprise. My boat is often pushed around, and jostled, though currents have never thrown me over. In general, the ebb or flood current is steady, though the water runs faster in the deep channel, and fastest around land that inserts itself into the flow, like the end of Magdalen Island. The speed of the current in my reach runs from slack to a little more than two knots. At slack there is little movement, which seems unnatural—a river should be moving.

The speed of water is measured in knots. A knot equals one nautical mile per hour (no such thing as knots per hour). And a nautical mile equals one minute of latitude at the equator, or rather one minute if the earth were perfectly round, which it is not. The simple translation of this is that a nautical mile is approximately 1.2 miles. Reading a nautical chart is easy: one minute on a chart equals one nautical mile. I keep my chart of the river in a plastic cover, strapped to the deck of my boat. On it I read where the channel runs, and avoid that, except when I need to cross. And, I can see how far I have traveled, and calculate how long it will take to get me home.

Knots were originally measured by using a rope with a piece of wood at the end. The Dutch started this in the 1500s using a technique they called, charmingly, "heaving the log." That technique was refined to the "chip log" technique, where a log attached to a rope was tossed overboard. The rope had knots spaced every fifty feet, and as the rope unwound, an hourglass measuring every thirty seconds timed the speed. It wasn't just our sixteenth-century cousins who did this; the U.S. Navy used a chip log technique as late as 1917.

◊ ◊ ◊

"Do you cross the river at night?" Carol asked.

I hadn't. But it was the thing to do. We ferried the width of the river in the last licks of light, passed the Saugerties Lighthouse, and ducked into the Esopus. The oily darkness of the creek was mysterious with black-on-black shadows obscuring abandoned docks that lurk below the surface of the water. We paddled by smell, until the lights from the marina gave us some purchase. A man and woman in kayaks zoomed in from behind us, slashing the water. They were impressed we'd crossed the river, as they had yet to leave the comfort of the Esopus. They lived on a few communal acres by the Esopus and swam in this tributary daily.

"We don't know anything about kayaking," he explained.

I liked both their enthusiasm and caution.

"You have to cross back, don't you?" she asked.

We did. I knew this was not the most sensible thing to do. We huddled together on the western shore, looking north and south for traffic. We had both attached lights to the sterns of our boats. The ten-inch-high rod, topped with a bright white 360-degree light, offered but the faintest signal we were there. But this was all the light required of kayaks on the river. Bigger boats need to be marked more clearly: red to port, green to starboard, and white lights for the bow and stern. Tugs display additional lights, the combination of white, yellow, and red lights indicating if they are pulling, pushing, or pulling alongside a barge.

I felt as if we were two kids doing something we knew we should not do. The lights on the Kingston Bridge dotted the far horizon. The stars blinked, complicit in our adventure.

"Let's stick together," I said, admitting a smidgen of fear.

That night, the current with us at two knots and the wind calm, we sped across the river. The thrill and worry of a possible barge emerging from the dark generated a surge of adrenalin. This is what I learned: speed depends on the current and wind, as well as on adrenalin and effort. But how you experience speed and distance depends on light, on what you can see. Knots at night are not the same as knots in daylight. At night, heading south with two knots of ebb, movement is imperceptible. At night, heading south with two knots of ebb, movement is smooth, and slick. It is delicious.

9

I'M GLAD YOU ARE HERE

When we arrived at the care center for dinner at 5:30 we had two gifts with us. One was lobster bisque made by a good friend. We were excited to have something that was also delicious to feed Jacquie. She took in small spoonfuls.

"C'est bon?" we asked after a few sips.

She nodded her head without hesitation.

My mother fed me. This is how I know love. Make me a meal, and I will know that you love me. We had been feeding my mother. Or trying to. In early August, Becky flew in from France. Our father had written an e-mail saying, "If you want to see your mother one last time, come." For three weeks we were together, our small, four-square family. My father had moved her to a care facility, with the innocuous name Atrium, where nurses tended to her in ways he no longer could. There, in her small, sunlit room, we sat at my mother's bedside.

In between visits we took walks, or, in the later afternoon, swam in the outdoor pool on campus. It sounds almost peaceful, but it was not. We were all riddled with anxiety, walking the halls at home through the night, sitting at the kitchen table eating cinnamon toast or bowls of cereal at odd hours.

My mother was no longer allowed to eat bread because the doctors worried about her suffocating on a crumb gone astray. No bread? Nothing could be worse for a French woman who used to show up at dinner parties with her own loaf, just in case. It was awful feeding her what she did not want, the mashed potatoes that had no flavor, the pureed beets, so orange-red but still tasteless. When I offered her a spoonful of chocolate pudding, I said, "It comes from Chez Pons," to entice her. Pons was her favorite tearoom in Paris.

"Pons," she corrected me.

I had not pronounced the *s* strongly enough. I smiled. She would never stop correcting my French.

We had some foie gras that Becky had smuggled in from France, made from ducks raised in Estampes. We gave her small spoonfuls of the rich duck liver, and she would smile at the familiar flavor, then ask, "Cracker?"

"No, no crackers." To say no broke my heart.

How else could we show our love? We sat by her bedside. We read her letters from friends. We told her of phone calls from those who loved her. Then Becky showed her the page proofs for her latest book, a history of girls' education in nineteenth-century France. She had dedicated the book to our mother. If Becky lived in, loved, and studied France, it was because of our mother. I cried watching Becky explain the dedication. Jacquie watched, attentive, but it wasn't clear how much she understood.

While we stood, alternately searching for things to say or do, the woman from across the hall called, "Help, help!" I looked into the hallway.

One of the strong, kind nurses strolled into her room. "What's wrong, Marguerite?" she asked.

"Nothing."

"Then you must stop yelling."

Two minutes later, Marguerite's cries resumed: "Help me! Help!"

"Marguerite, you're yelling again."

"I'm not yelling," she said.

"Yes, you are. I can hear you all the way down the hall. You must stop yelling."

Before leaving my mother's room we all held hands. This was a ritual my parents had started with Becky's children to settle them into dinner. I'm glad you are here, you say to the person next to you, and then that person turns to the next, passing on the same gladness. My mother said, "I'm glad you are here, Susie." More words than she'd said in days.

I kissed her. "I love you, my little mother."

"I love you, my," and she hesitated, "big daughter." A bit of a laugh emerged, and we joined her.

As we gathered to leave, my father stopped and turned, as if he'd forgotten something. "I miss you. I wish you were still at home." The three of us held hands and wept as we walked down the hallway.

"Help, help me!" echoed down the hall behind us.

We broke from tears to laughter.

On the way home our father said, "I don't know how I'll adjust to living alone."

Living alone was what I had done for so long that living with someone would be an adjustment for me. Still, I understood my father's fears, as I had my daily rituals that helped to keep the loneliness at bay. I was quick to give my father advice: Make sure you get out every day. Speak to one person face to face. You can't rely on the phone, you have to see one other person. Make real meals—no bowls of cereal for dinner—and don't eat standing at the kitchen counter.

He confessed he was afraid he would get into bad routines, up late watching movies, or that he would go out every night for dinner and entertain others by telling stories. "I should just hole up and write," he said. In June his novel *Jerry Engels* had gotten over-the-top reviews in the Sunday edition of the *New York Times Book Review* and in the *New York Review of Books*. If he had not been tending to my mother, those reviews would have sent him sailing into his next book. Instead the first four chapters of the new manuscript remained an unopened file on his computer desktop while he played endless games of solitaire, figured out Sudoku puzzles, or watched reruns of *Casablanca.*

◊ ◊ ◊

On August 26, Jacquie was writhing in pain. I would take her hand to soothe her, but she cringed at my touch, her skin brittle, seemingly on fire. Early in the day, I had begged the nurses for more morphine for her. There was nothing they could do, the nurses explained. At a certain point, when the organs begin to shut down, the morphine does no good, doesn't circulate soothingly in the system.

So we sat, or paced, and watched. We had made the choice, my father, sister, and I, not to take any medical interventions. My father and I had signed the papers, tears flowing down our cheeks. We knew there was no other choice, but I wished then that something could be done. Watching her pain was agony.

At seven in the evening, I insisted we leave. My father—exhausted from weeks at my mother's bedside—needed to eat and to rest.

I stood at the end of her bed and mouthed, but did not say loud enough for anyone to hear, "You can go, Mama, we'll be OK." And I realized there, that though we had pretended to care for her, all along she was still caring for us. She was hanging on for us.

◊ ◊ ◊

It was still dark when my cell phone rang next to my bed.

"Susan," the nurse said, "you should come." She paused. A voice echoed in the background. "Oh. Your mother just died."

I got up, walked barefoot down the hall to my parents' bedroom. I was a child again, rushing to my father, hoping he would make things better.

I opened the door without knocking.

"Mama's dead." I said.

He sat up, white hair disheveled and without a word opened his arms. He held me, his body still warm and soft with sleep.

A week later, we had an Episcopal service for Jacquie, though she was a Christmas and Easter Catholic. The ritual of the service comforted us, and my mother got her wish: that people did not stand up and talk about what a wonderful little lady she was, how cute she was on her bicycle as she ran her errands around town.

We read "Recueillement" by Baudelaire and "Le cimetière marin" by Paul Valéry. In the poem was the line she had so often repeated: "Il faut tenter de vivre!"

You must commit life.

IO

THE LONG LONELINESS

Too soon, I was back in Tivoli, back to teaching, back on the river. I was grateful for my students, who appeared in my office full of questions about their essays, puzzling over both their ideas and their sentence fragments. Unaware of my grief, they carried on with their imagined futures before them. Their energy pulled me out of myself. And I was grateful for the river that, like my students, continued its steady flow. In the evenings or on weekends I needed to feel the stir of water beneath me.

I didn't paddle; I drifted, flowing with the current. I was aimless, cut loose. If the current carried me north from Tivoli a few hundred yards I landed below Rose Hill. The cement wall below the house had fresh graffiti; no longer did *Jane love's Harry.* How could someone write over that *love's?* Now there were fat black and white letters that I could not decipher.

I had always been drawn to Rose Hill; it is a beautiful brick house with a fascinating history. Between 1964 and 1979, the visionary Dorothy Day established one of her Catholic Worker homes in the house and the outbuildings. The goal of the worker movement was to meld socialist ideas with the teachings within the Catholic Church. For Day this meant feeding and tending to the poor. Solace for our suffering, whether physical, emotional, or spiritual, could be found in community. In community, we might escape our loneliness. In her autobiography, *The Long Loneliness*, Day writes: "I was lonely, deadly lonely. And I was to find out then, as I found out so many times, over and over again, that women especially are social beings, who are not content with just husband and family, but must have a community, a group, an exchange with others. A child is not enough. A husband and children, no matter how busy one may be kept by them, are not enough." For me, nothing felt enough. So as I floated beneath Rose Hill, I used the house in which Day worked as an emotional beacon, guiding me as I paddled toward my own solace, toward my own understanding of *love's*.

I was nineteen and wrestling with life when my therapist placed Day's autobiography in my hands. I am not Catholic, but Day's spiritual life spoke to the young me. Now I turned to Day again, but not to her writings. I was fascinated with her life. Day, like most women, felt the pull of family, but her ideas on liberation for women took her elsewhere. She was jailed and took part in a hunger strike when she was arrested for marching for women's right to vote. And then she made the bold choice to live in community with the poor, raise her daughter alone, and in this way devote her life to God. I saw that such a life requires courage.

What brought Day to this house by the river? I like to imagine she moved to Rose Hill because she loved the river, though I doubt that was her motivation. Perhaps it was because the house was a bargain— $175,000 for sixty acres and a large run-down house with outbuildings. I did not come to Tivoli for the river either. I came for work, to teach at Bard College. And yet the river had seeped into my life so fast, so naturally. When I spoke about my kayak outings, I caught myself saying, "I love the Hudson River." And I wondered if it was possible to love a river. Or rather, why was I spending so much time loving something when I knew for sure I would not be loved in return? Though this sort of love was safe: there was no chance of being rejected, there was no chance of being left. The river would be there. As one-sided as it was, this love would help as I started to orient myself in a world where a love I was sure of, a love I had counted on, was gone.

◊ ◊ ◊

Rose Hill has seen many lives. General John Watts de Peyster and Estelle Livingston built the house in 1843. Both were heirs to great fortunes. He managed to put his name on several buildings in town, including the firehouse (now the village hall) and the Watts de Peyster Industrial Home for Girls. In 1892 he also built the Methodist Church in the middle of town. Despite this résumé of building good buildings, one local historian has nothing kind to say about de Peyster. Estelle brought to the marriage the Livingston name. Livingston is not just a Hudson River name. From the seventeenth to the nineteenth century, the Livingstons were one of America's great aristocratic families. The Livingstons who arrived in the seventeenth century acquired as much land as possible. At one point the central estate ran from the river to the Massachusetts border and covered a million acres—an expanse of land the size of the state of Rhode Island. The view from many of the Livingston mansions spread west into the Catskills, where they owned acres of forested mountains.

Following the Livingston story is fascinating but challenging, as in every generation they name an heir Robert (I count sixty-three); there are two Robert Robert Livingstons as well. The lack of imagination in naming is dazzling: there is a Livingston Livingston tucked in there, lest the young man forget his origins.

The early Livingstons were politically ambitious. Robert R. became a New York Supreme Court justice (he was known as Robert "the Judge"), and his son Robert R. Junior (known as Robert "the Chancellor") administered the oath of office to George Washington and signed the Declaration of Independence. He later became minister to France and helped to negotiate the Louisiana Purchase. Robert R. Junior also collaborated with Fulton in the construction of the steamboat. And yet in these major events the Livingston name is often forgotten. Livingston is not credited with the Louisiana Purchase—didn't we learn in school that it was James Monroe?—because Livingston changed the dates on important documents, nullifying much of his hard work. And shortly after the steamboat was launched, Robert got into financial tangles with Fulton, which marred the final years of his life.

After these years of public service by the Roberts, the Livingston family largely retreated from public life to enjoy their beautiful views of the Hudson Valley. They kept to themselves, marrying with other members of prominent families, the Beekmans or the Van Rensselaers. A tour of big houses from Rhinecliff north would involve stops at up to forty homes connected to the Livingston fortune.

Some historians make out the Livingstons to be lazy and greedy. Regardless of their character, I do have to thank the Livingstons—a Livingston granted land to Tivoli's dreamy creator, de Labigarre. And many Livingston properties are now parks, open to the public. Though some Livingston heirs still cling to their homes, many, battered by high taxes, have given their properties to New York State. A few miles north of Tivoli is Clermont State Park, site of the main Livingston home. Keeping track of the homes can be as difficult as keeping track of the Livingstons themselves; houses burned at an alarming rate. Most of these fires were those of the times—set by lamps, the heating stove, or in one instance a spark from a passing coal train. The original house at Clermont was razed by British forces in the Revolutionary War. The house was rebuilt, and the land around it offers trails through old hardwood forests. It is one of my favorite places to walk.

◊ ◊ ◊

De Peyster left Rose Hill to serve as an orphanage for boys. Orphaned girls lived in the middle of town at the de Peyster Industrial Home, which stayed in operation into the mid-twentieth century. Two orphanages in a village that has never had a population much greater than 1,500 is hard to imagine. But many state institutions meant to serve New York City, such as prisons and psychiatric wards, were built in this region. After a series of owners, a successful painter bought

Rose Hill. Under his care, the house looks content, secretive, perhaps a bit lonely.

That one house could move from sheltering the wealthy to orphans to Catholic radicals, and now an artist, is a story that, with variation, can be told throughout the valley. I like to think of those years when Rose Hill served the poor as an antidote to the Livingston greed. Over and over again, the river has been able to redeem itself—from sewage dump to a nearly clean river. Or if not redemption, then at least there has been transformation. So too for those of us who dwell on its banks.

Dorothy Day was a woman of transformation. This is one reason I admire her so. In her young life she lived as a bohemian in New York City, and it is no secret that she got pregnant and had an abortion long before it was legal. She fictionalized her story in a novel, *The Eleventh Virgin.* She spent her later life trying to destroy the book; few original editions remain, though a handful of libraries hold photocopies.

The Eleventh Virgin has all the marks of a first novel. It is a sexual coming-of-age story, laced with fervent discussions about a woman's role in the home, sexual freedom, socialism, and God. It covers a lot of territory. The central character, June, like Day herself, is jailed for marching for women's rights. Later she falls in love with a young radical, Dick Wemys, and gives over everything for him, sitting at home as he pursues his acting career. The only thing he promises her is that he'll leave. Still, she clings to him, despite her feminist thoughts. Day concludes the novel with June declaring: "I know what I want. It's Dick and marriage and babies! And I'll have them yet. Wait and see." This pull between independence, pursuing her ideas and freedom, and the imperative to mate is June's struggle. It was Day's struggle. This is not a new story, but for every woman who wrestles with this choice, it is never easy. Ideas are powerful, so is biology.

When I think of how I have engaged in this struggle, I think of the river's movement in and out with the tides. I've gone back and forth, insisting on my independence, then giving over to a relationship, a more domestic life. Despite my will toward independence, there is the inevitable pull toward home. The inevitable desire to love and be loved.

Like Day, I have had my own transformations, though most are small. I dream of a big change, the one where I pack up to work in the Antarctic, move to the southwest of France to live off the land, or sell everything and hit the road in an Airstream. But most of my transformations require rewinding the clock more than a few years. The one where I marry and have a pack of children, live in a rambling house. Or else the life where I travel to Nepal and climb big mountains. What I want in all of these transformations is a commitment to one thing, a focus that runs deep. But I have lived my life split: between France and the United States, between books and adventure, between men and women. Whatever I have done, wherever I have lived, whomever I have loved, I have always had one foot out the door, one eye on the horizon. Now, in the wake of my mother's death the urge to root was overwhelming. I wanted to commit to a place, a life, a job, a person. I wanted the force of those choices to feel like being pulled out to sea.

Was it possible for me to make such a change? Day gave me hope that any change was possible. When Day turned to the Catholic Church it looks as if she knew what that meant, was consumed by a powerful faith. But her doubt is evident in her journal writings, which appear in Day's work *On Pilgrimage.* This hesitation reminds me that no one understands fully her own life; we all live with doubt. The point is to make a choice and stick with it.

For me, the pivotal moment for Day was when she baptized her daughter. The father—a committed anarchist—wanted nothing to do with the church. So Day's choice was for her love of God over an earthly love. She made this choice full of an intelligent doubt, and she stuck to her decision. She chose the life she led. We all choose our lives, though it was sometimes easier for me to believe that I had ended up alone on the Hudson River by accident.

Day found relief for her loneliness in community, in sharing the suffering—of the spirit but also of hunger—with others. That is what we did after my mother's death. We phoned everyone who had ever loved her and had long conversations, filled with tears, laughter, memories of meals and beaches and trips to France. Remember when. Remember when. Yes, yes, so much was good. So much was sad. We did not talk of what was unfulfilled, left undone. The inarticulate emptiness was sadness enough.

Then we had a fine party, with Kentucky ham and salmon flown in from the Pacific Northwest, a mousse de foie gras, wine, and cheese. The house was mobbed. Cards poured in; enormous bouquets of flowers scented every room. Jacquie would have loved it all.

But now, back to my life in Tivoli, I was looking for relief in solitude, in movement, and by entering the natural world. There, in early September, I needed the river as I never had before.

II

SOLACE

It was mid-September when I awakened in my friend Emily's tent, my sleeping bag bunched around my legs, sticky with the sweat of sleep. The sun was beginning to make the yellow walls of our shelter vibrate with life. We had landed and set up camp in the dark, so, curious to see what surrounded us, I unzipped the tent door. It folded to the ground, an arc framing my view. Mist rose like a halo over the water. It looked otherworldly, though it was easy to explain—the air was cooler than the water. A beige and black expanse of sand skidded to the water's edge, and the water there did not move. This stillness, a cousin to silence, was why I had ventured out on this overnight on the Hudson River. Camping pulls my soul together.

"Em," I said softly, nudging her awake, "look at this." It was important someone else saw what I saw; to hoard such a vision would be selfish. Also, to share is to not feel as alone.

"Em." I rocked my hip into hers, my weight resting for a moment as incentive for her to move. It was an intimate gesture, though we are just friends. "You have to see this." She bolted up, shaggy with sleep,

her short, wavy brown hair half covering her clear eyes. Her smooth
face had the softness of sleep.

She peered out onto the world. "Wow," she said. That's all there
was to say.

It was to be a simple-enough outing: put in at Stockport Flats,
paddle five miles north to Bronck Island, camp, and, in the morning,
head back. That's not what happened. Life and kayaking trips just are
not that simple. To want that is to yearn against the tides.

The day before, at four in the afternoon, Emily and I had driven
down winding Station Road, which follows Stockport Creek, to the
gravel parking lot by the railroad tracks. Just before the lot we passed
the Staats House, built between 1654 and 1664. Ten years to build a
modest stone house. A sign told us that Henry Hudson had landed at
this spot on September 17, 1609. In fact, this was where Hudson had
his first meal on land in the New World. In one of the rare fragments
from Hudson's own journal we learn that he was served food in "red
wooden bowls." The natives fed him pigeons, and "they likewise killed
a fat dog, and skinned it in great haste, with shells which they had
got out of the water." That pigeon and dog meal was almost exactly
396 years earlier. In some ways that was so little time; yet all that had
been built, cut down, dug up, plowed under, or burned on this parcel
of land was hard to imagine.

Some of the differences between the river that Henry Hudson saw
and the river we now know are obvious—the railroad, all of the grand
mansions looking down onto the water, and the industry on shore.
Other differences are less known—there were heath hens, now ex-
tinct, and mountain lions, the last one shot in the 1850s. It is perhaps
for the mountain lion that the Catskills are named: the "cat's river."
But like many names in the Hudson Valley, the origin of the name
Catskills is unclear, and there are many explanations. There were also
thousands of beaver in the river. By one estimate, 80,000 beaver were
killed *annually* in the seventeenth century. The forests were dominated
by oak, chestnut, and hickory. Now our forests have declined, with the
chestnut infected with chestnut blight and oak diminished by oak wilt.
Dutch elm disease has taken most of our elms. Fish then were plenti-
ful and not laden with toxins.

Yet Robert Boyle writes that the most basic difference between now and then is smell. Then, it was "marvelously fragrant," while now we breathe in the "noxious stinks of oil, gas, chemicals, and industrial wastes." Robert Juet writes on September 6: "The lands they told us were as pleasant with grass and flowers, and goodly trees, as ever they had seen, and very sweet smells came from them." Of course, as compared to the smells on ship, which were a potent mixture of unwashed men and whatever they carried below deck—including live animals—any smell would be sweet. But later explorers also were taken with the smells of the valley. In the 1700s, the Dutchman Adriaen van der Donck wrote: "The air in the New-Netherlands is so dry, sweet and healthy, that we need not wish it were otherwise. In purity, agreeableness, and fineness, it would be folly to seek for an example of it in any other country." Today, the smell that emerges from the river is at times sweet. There are those moments in spring when the honeysuckle is in bloom. Or midsummer when the spice bush bears fruit. But most days there's a mixture of odors, dominated by creosote and oil. Often these smells are overwhelmed by the rot of a deer killed by a passing train or a dead fish basking in the sun. At low tide the mud that forms the compost for the river offers up an odor that bites at the back of the throat. All of these smells—natural and unnatural—combine to make a curious, often unpleasant potpourri. What would it take to return to that sweet smell of the 1700s?

What I imagine has changed the most, however, are the sounds on the river. When I think it is quiet, there is in fact some noise: a boat in the distance, the horn of the train, or the clank of steel against steel on the rails. There is a subtle drone that comes from the traffic on the roads that line the river or from an airplane overhead. Our endless movement creates unceasing noise.

◊ ◊ ◊

Emily and I unloaded our kayaks and placed them in the water. At low tide, rocks emerged in the familiar river muck, which sucked at our aqua socks. As we stuffed dry bags into the hatches, I told her I had remembered the pesto and Parmesan cheese, and milk for coffee, but had forgotten the coffee itself. Emily looked like she might not forgive me.

Since my mother's death, Emily stopped every morning for a cup of coffee from my espresso machine. Seated on a wooden bench on my front porch, we discussed our day, politics, or books read, while she rolled a cigarette. This morning ritual helped to keep me anchored as I floated in my grief.

It was Emily and her sister who had pulled me into the winter night and down to the river when I first arrived in Tivoli. Since that time, she and I had shared some adventures. We had climbed Slide Mountain, the highest peak in the Catskills, one winter day when the temperature hit negative 20. On the summit, we took photos of her long, frozen eyelashes. The previous summer, we had traveled to Alaska and flown into the Wrangell Mountains in a two-seater plane. For six days we trekked through remote, beautiful country, carrying heavy plastic bear canisters in which to keep our food safe from grizzlies. So here we were on the Hudson, looking for a bit of local outdoor exploration. I saw being coffeeless as adding to the adventure.

We pushed into Stockport Creek and under the railroad bridge, a long, steel-framed bridge, the red girders forming a tunnel for the rushing trains. Out on the river, the rounded tip of Stockport Island lay a quarter mile north. The island, along with Gay's Point to the north, is part of the Hudson River Islands State Park. Both islands were created from dredge spoil. Dredge spoil is river dirt. In the 1930s, 1940s, and 1950s, the U.S. Army Corps of Engineers deepened the commercial shipping channel to thirty feet or more. That displaced soil was dumped along the banks of the river, and over time grass, shrubs, and trees have grown. Cottonwoods and locust trees like the sandy soil from the riverbed. One study estimates that over the years as much as 7,000 acres have been added to the shoreline and as islands due to dredge from the river.

On Stockport Island, beaches meet the water. Lopsided picnic benches, as well as a few campsites, rest amidst the thick forest. The current was nominally with us; the wind was utterly against us. The result was a chop, the water knocking us around, so that we both were soon damp from spray. It was rough enough that we needed to focus, not meander and talk. The river was wide, empty, isolated.

The river, in other words, reflected how I felt, which, despite friends and daily calls from my father or sister, was more alone than ever. Three weeks after my mother's death, I was awash in that aloneness. Raw with the need for love and human connection, I had veered toward the opposite, isolating myself. The isolation was creating its own space inside me, a hole within the hole created by my mother's absence. Something had to fill that hole, like water pouring toward low ground. The question was what? Dirt, concrete, water, wood, tears?

As we crossed the river to the western shore, we passed a square green sign on a metal tower, which marked the western boundary of the shipping channel. My chart told me the marker flashed every four seconds at night. Red markers indicate the eastern edge of deep water. I chant "red, right, return" in order to remember this. This refrain is critical for captains of bigger boats as they return to port—red buoys should be on their right. Straying from the channel can mean running aground or worse.

This was a rare spot along the river, the train tracks on both shores inland, making our travels more peaceful. A row of houses trails south out of Coxsackie (pronounced Cook-sackie; the name is Algonquian and translates as "owl hoot"). Each house faces the river; docks of wood or steel run into the water. Larger boats were tied to the docks; canoes and kayaks were stored on shore.

If the houses of Coxsackie open to the river, the town turns its back on the river. We could not see over the steel breakwater to the flat lawn of the town park and the parking area. All we could see was the top of the nearest building, a tall barnlike brick structure, which had long, boarded-up windows.

An aluminum walkway led down to a floating wooden dock that stretched along the shoreline for thirty feet. There, a woman fished indifferently.

"Do you know if there is a deli in town?" I asked.

She shrugged. "I'm not from here."

Neither of us wanted to get out of our boats to search for coffee. The sun was tilting over the sloping horizon; we felt an urgency to find our campsite.

We passed on the western side of Coxsackie Island, skimming along a marina where several dozen motorboats rocked, moored to floating docks. I settled into a slow stroke, reminding myself, as I rotated side to side, to reach. My boat listed to the right, and I leaned, sweeping my paddle to correct for this. Kayaking is often counterintuitive. To keep a true course, you have to lean into the problem. *Immerse yourself in your aloneness, and the aloneness will right itself,* I thought as I skimmed along the water.

We passed through an opening about 300 feet wide between shore and the island. Around us was undeveloped forest. A pileated woodpecker laughed at us from the nearby woods; ring-billed gulls swooped across the river, making their gymnastic tilts and dives; a fish leapt, its splash startling me.

We passed Ratttlesnake Island and, two miles north, glided onto the sand beach at Bronck Island. The *Hudson River Water Trail Guide* makes Bronck, which is not a true island, sound like an ideal place to camp, since the land is accessible only from the water. "Watch out for poison ivy," the guide advises. Despite the head wind, we had arrived just at nightfall to set up camp.

As I pulled back my spray skirt to slip out of my boat, boys on ATVs roared out of the darkness. They spun onto the sand beach before heading back into the woods. I looked at Emily, and we both shook our heads. Not a place for two women to set up camp. So as the sun surely set and vanished, leaving us dipping our paddles in the dark water, we turned south looking for a place to pitch a tent.

How does a person find solace? I thought of Day in her loneliness creating community. But what I reached for now was not a hug or a sympathetic pat on the back. I worried that those gestures would mask my feelings. I wanted to feel my sadness in all of its force; I wanted to be knocked around, brought into life by being pushed open. My way to solace was by feeling more vigorously the pain and un-simpleness of life, then finding a place big and open enough to contain it. Other attempts at solace—a numbing drink, a swathe of kisses, or a good meal—might help, but they felt like Band-Aids, momentary comforts. And yet a good meal was my mother's best defense against sadness. She was an inspired cook. The night before as I blended the basil and garlic, added more Parmesan and oil, I thought, *She would like this dinner.*

I was thinking about that pesto as darkness took over. I was hungry, and tired—the wind was exhausting. And now the night, which can be so soothing, had set my nerves afire. We hugged the shore, avoiding the lights of the few remaining boats churning on their way back to Coxsackie. As we groped our way along the east side of the island we ran into reed grass and tangles of trees that made landing impossible. My eyes strained to see, and even with the faint glow of my headlamp I could not distinguish what was a good landing or not. Suddenly Emily was out of her boat, across a log and stomping through the "ozie" ground.

"Here's a spot," she said, her voice flat with fatigue. We moved silently in tandem, Emily setting up the tent, me tending to food, both of us inflating Therm-a-Rests, unfolding sleeping bags. Soon enough we were eating, spooning in mouthfuls of the garlic- and basil-coated pasta. Afterward, sleep came easily in the still, soft tent.

◊ ◊ ◊

The beauty of the beach was more tonic than any cup of coffee, and we walked, adding our soft prints to those of a deer, a raccoon. Soon, we packed our reluctant boats and paddled to Coxsackie, where I promised Emily there had to be a coffee shop where the locals ate breakfast. We wandered into town, the large brick buildings enchanting, tilting back to a rich past. One building had an elaborate series of wooden porches; on the second floor, a few people sat drinking coffee. They waved good morning. What they saw was two women in shorts and long-sleeved shirts carrying their paddles, hair a bit of a mess.

Downtown Coxsackie is, like so many upriver towns, desperate to come back to life. It was hard to know what people lived off of. Many of the large industries in the valley have shut down. IBM closed in Kingston years ago, leaving many jobless. In Coxsackie the big employer had been the American Valve Plant, which closed in 1986 after seventy years of operation. The end of these industrial employers is a relief for the environment, for the river, but shutting these plants had hurt the town economically.

Starbucks may never land in this town, but we found a lively coffee shop where they sold us watery coffee. It was hot and that was all I needed. I caught snippets of conversations and for a moment envied the man with his two sons eating pancakes in the far corner. From a distance, his life looked neat.

We walked back to our boats, crossing a grass opening. A man wearing a T-shirt that showed he worked for the town was collecting garbage from a can.

"Has there always been a park here?" I asked.

"Always. And I grew up here." He was perhaps in his forties. "The gazebo there," he pointed to a round white gazebo on the far end of a grass lawn, "that was smashed when the icebergs came off the river."

"Icebergs?" I asked.

"Ran it up against that building." He pointed to the bricklike barn, which sat 200 feet away. "They say they let the water out of the dam too early in the season, before the ice cleared out."

That would be the Troy dam. I nodded. "Thanks," I said.

We strolled over to the gazebo. There we learned it was built in 1987 and rebuilt after the ice storms and floods of 1996. It was hard, on such a clear, summer day to imagine the violence of such a storm. And though the man blamed the severity on the dam release, there are accounts beginning in the seventeenth century (long before the dam, which was built in 1823) of high freshets that flooded islands. In later years, these floods caused a range of damage, including drowning train tracks. (By contrast, the lower half of the estuary does not flood.)

On the dock, the sun now in full force, we sipped our coffee. Emily asked, "Why isn't everyone out here?" It was something I wondered all the time. How is it that people are not drawn out, to the edges of this river or onto it, seeking pleasure, adventure, calm, and solace? But I was grateful they were not here. The peace the river offers would be shattered if people flocked outdoors to fish or paddle.

On the far shore we could see a brick tower rising from the trees. Drawn to it, we found there at Nutton Hook the remains of an icehouse. There are four ornate brick walls with no roof, and a tall chimney stack. A cottonwood sapling grew out of the top of that chimney stack, and the walls were surrounded by bushes and thin red maples, taking over where industry left off. This tower powered the lifts that brought blocks of ice off the river and raised them into a huge wooden building that measured 200 by 300 feet and stood 40 feet tall. It could hold 52,880 tons of ice.

Photos of ice harvesting show horses plodding onto the thick frozen river, dragging sleds that cleared off the snow. Channels were cut, and in them the blocks floated toward shore. They were then heaved by machine up and into the icehouses. During the nineteenth century there were 135 icehouses on the river, most in this section, between Catskill and Albany, keeping up to 20,000 men busy in season. From here in the upper part of the Hudson three million tons of ice were shipped by barge and train to New York City and at times as far away as India or the Caribbean. This icehouse closed in 1934. The large, windowless building was perfect for growing mushrooms, which is what one entrepreneur did until the building burned down. Now, cottonwoods have taken to that rich soil, growing tall and strong. Their puffs of "cotton" shed in the spring, floating about like fluffy snowflakes.

As we loitered by the former icehouse, a tanker floated south, its name in large red letters: *Accurate*. Like many boat names—*So Little Time, Sanctuary, Dreamer*—it told a lot about the owner. This name becomes a command: be accurate. I felt it impossible to be accurate about my sense of loss and loneliness. On a scale of one to ten it was so past a ten that I'd lost perspective.

What I could be clear about was all the ways the river had offered solace: in the smells and sounds, the wind and waves. There was comfort in the level ground where we had slept, and in the pull of the river, so sure, like Emily's friendship. How grateful I was for that steadiness. The river and Emily together had tugged me just a bit from my isolation.

Heading south, there was that familiar pleasure of nothing happening. We rounded Gay's Point, waved to the picnickers at Stockport Middle Ground, glided under the bridge, and slid out of the water to our car, waiting in the parking lot.

12

LEARNING THE RIVER

The sight of a tug shoving or towing a barge delights me. Tugs are so small, so lively, often painted in bright colors, that it is hard not to use the word *cheerful* when describing them. They push or pull the long heavy barges north and south against the current and in all weather with such purpose, even tenacity. This gives them character. Beyond how endearing they are, tugs also remind me that this is a working river and that the work of the river is moving stuff—oil, junked cars, a huge range of building supplies. The only time a tug isn't an endearing sight is when I am in a kayak and a tug is pushing a barge straight at me.

I'm not sure why I didn't see the *Virginia C.* as I crossed the river from Beacon to Plum Point. The river at this section is a little over a mile wide, with long views north toward the Beacon-Newburgh Bridge and south into the Highlands. I'd been scanning the horizon, attentive to the movement on the river, because this was a section I had paddled but once before, with Emmet.

It was April of 2006. I had decided this was the summer I would explore the river, drive north and south and put my boat in the water to see what I might see. The new landscape would jolt me out of my comfortable, sad paddles in my reach. I could hear my mother approving this look forward.

My friend John Cronin listened to my resolve to explore and suggested that I come paddle out of Beacon. "I'll help you get your boat in the water and come get you in Manitou," he offered.

It was the sort of plan I spend hours trying to orchestrate. Though I claim that going out and coming back are not the same—views shift, and the heron that took flight on the out will have vanished on the return, replaced perhaps by a bald eagle overhead—there's a simple satisfaction in just heading out, covering miles in a stretch, without calculating for the return. In this case, it was a fourteen-mile shot south. Despite all of this encouragement, I had had to force myself out the door to drive one hour south. Venturing out of my reach felt a bit dangerous.

So there I was in my wet suit, armor against the cold water below me. And there was the barge, looming out of the south, its rusted gray-brown hull riding high in the water, a wall of steel almost indistinguishable in color from the rusty-green-brown water. The snout of the tug, painted a vibrant red, peeked above the barge from behind. All of this, impossibly near.

It is difficult to gauge speed and distance on water. And it's also hard to tell if a boat is heading right toward you or not. But from my water-level view there was no question the barge was bearing down on me. I knew this because it was close, not more than 200 yards away. A barge can't stop and it can't swerve. It was up to me to stay out of the way, either by sprinting toward shore and squirting past or by veering sharply south, keeping to the middle of the river until the barge surged past. I chose the latter.

To ride down the middle of the Hudson where it is wide, where there's plenty of boat traffic, and you are small and slow moving—this is to be exposed. Clutching my paddle more firmly than I needed, I stroked south. Within moments the barge and tug passed, the force of their deep speed grazing my right shoulder. The captain of the tug stood on deck; I thought I saw him shake his head before stepping back into the cabin. I imagined he was relieved, but mostly irritated. I have heard that tug captains refer to kayakers as "speed bumps." I felt foolish. I should have seen the barge, but the sun high in the sky, the color of the boat, and that of the water had all worked against me. The big, rolling waves from the wake of the barge rocked my kayak. Once I caught my breath, I darted for shore. I limped out of my boat on Plum Point, where a gaggle of men had their fishing poles stuck in the water. I had crossed the river because of Plum Point—it was one of those place-names that had sparked my imagination. Yet there wasn't much to Plum Point—a few hardwood trees and some picnic tables—that made me need to stay long.

My wet suit rubbed against my skin, clammy in the heat of the late morning. My boat was heavy; in the hatches I had stored enough clothing and food for a week on the river. By midsummer I would be heading out with hatches empty except for a jug of water and sunscreen. Vigilance would give over to the casualness of hot air and warm water. For now, though, I was prepared for anything. Except my own stupidity.

I pulled out my cell phone. "I almost got run over by a barge," I reported without saying hello.

A beat of silence. "Boats do collide," John said.

◊ ◊ ◊

I had met John the summer before on the river during a program named River Summer. I was one of a dozen faculty living aboard the *Sea Wolf*, a research boat, as we learned about the Hudson River. I joined the boat in Catskill and stayed with it for ten days until it docked at Bear Mountain. During that time, the faculty on board pooled their knowledge about the river. A biologist had us peer through a microscope at the invasive zebra mussel and then told us how they clog intake pipes, while an environmental lawyer presented the history of Storm King. A geologist explained that the Hudson was a drowned river, a fjord filled with water. We helped a scientist take water samples to add to his data on the river's salinity, which has been measured as far north as Poughkeepsie, though the level of saltwater intrusion was normal to West Point. Led by an art historian, we hiked to the top of

Kaaterskill Falls and imagined ourselves Thomas Cole as we tried our hand at creating perspective with watercolors, charcoal, and ink. Led by a naturalist from the Audubon Center, we canoed into Constitution Marsh, then into Foundry Cove—the one a wildlife sanctuary, the other a Superfund site. In Foundry Cove, we took samples of soil from the area that used to be the dumping grounds for the Marathon Battery Company. When we were docked in Poughkeepsie we hired a cab to take us to Vassar College, where one of the River Summer participants taught chemistry. It was near eleven at night when he opened his lab for us. We took our samples and tested them for cadmium. That we found not even trace amounts was good news for the marsh, a successful rehabilitation project.

In the evenings, we sat on the deck of the boat, and I had everyone write about his or her experiences on the river. "Describe your first time on the river," I prompted. It took some encouragement to get lawyers or biologists to give over to narrative and personal reflection. For one day, John joined us, sharing his wealth of knowledge about the river.

I had never met John until then, but I had heard about his decades of work on the river. I had read his book, coauthored with Robert F. Kennedy, Jr., about his seventeen years at Riverkeeper. I had read profiles about him in a range of publications from *Time* magazine to the *New Yorker*. He's a man who attracts the media because he is articulate and imaginative about the environmental issues that we face. I also knew his reputation—that he was a man who went in for a fight.

When I met John for the first time that day on the dock in Cold Spring I thought he looked like a fighter. He is tall, and his arms swing at his side when he walks, large hands curled into a half fist. What I wasn't prepared for was his easygoing manner. For a man so busy, he dressed like he was on vacation. He wore shorts and a worn pair of Jack Purcells. His curly hair had hints of blond from the sun.

Soon after that first meeting, John and I had dinner. Our conversation ranged from Thomas Merton to John Steinbeck, and then eventually the river. I had rarely met a mind so elastic. What accounts for John's range lies in his past, which holds many chapters: there was the stint working for Maurice Hinchey in Albany; the seasons in the boats of legendary fisherman Bob Gabrielson, taking in shad and crab; his years living by the river in Manitou. There's no law school or formal environmental policy training in there, just common sense and vision and formidable energy.

◊ ◊ ◊

I looked back at the eastern shore, where I had launched but a half hour ago. As John had helped me with my boat, he had pulled a crab from a fisherman's pot, dangling from the side of the dock.

"Beautiful swimmer," he said. "That's what the Greek name means."

He showed me the difference between male and female crabs, the male having a long apron on its abdomen—a lighthouse shape—while the female is rounded. Blue crabs have red at the tips of their claws, "like red nail polish," he added with a grin.

From the small dock in Beacon I had pointed south, crossing the bay that cradles into Denning's Point. A year before, Emmet and I had crossed that bay together in the dark. Much had changed since then. I knew more about the river—the bay we crossed is called Biscuit Bay, for the Nabisco factory that once stood near shore. The factory printed Nabisco packaging like cereal boxes, and now has been transformed into an art museum, the Dia Foundation. On Denning's Point, where Emmet and I had camped, are the remains of a paper-clip factory. In the past year, I had wandered through the abandoned brick building, collecting rusted paper clips. At the northern end of the island is Beacon Institute's Center for Environmental Innovation and Education. The center's state-of-the-art building was originally part of a brick factory. From my years on the river, I knew a lot, and I knew how little I knew. A few years on a river is just enough time to become acquainted. This river time didn't discourage me; it made me want to learn more.

◊ ◊ ◊

On the river, looking south, was Pollopel Island; Bannerman's Castle was even more crumbled than when I had floated past a year ago.

Bannerman Castle Trust was hard at work trying to stabilize the structure. All of this was framed by Storm King on the west side and Breakneck Ridge on the east. Both mountains plunge to the river in a dramatic drop, the river surging below. It is this picture postcard view that makes people use words like "majestic" and "mighty," two words I would like to ban in relation to the river. The Hudson may indeed be majestic, but that one word flattens the complexity that I had come to know, the rich intertwining of beautiful and worn.

From my perspective the spring-muddy river ended just past Pollopel, came to a gentle horseshoe curve and stopped, forming a large lake. From the south, the bend in the river gives this same sense that the river ends, so it's no wonder that sailors first journeying up the river named this point World's End.

I continued south, and as I rounded Storm King I was on edge, unsure what to expect as the currents picked up in exciting ways, the water agitated as if I might be spit out into the narrow passage of the river.

If the river has a symbol or mascot it is Storm King Mountain. For twenty-seven years it was at the center of one of the most important environmental battles in this country. In 1963, Consolidated Edison, which supplied New York City's electricity, applied to build a pump storage station on the top of the mountain. The plant would suck up water and pump it to a storage reservoir. In times of electrical emergency, for instance summer brownouts, this water would be released, surging downhill through turbines that would create power for the city. It's an ingenious idea, in some ways. But it met with instant objection from those who love the beauty of the Highlands, as the plant would deface the mountain. Coupled with this were concerns for the environment, particularly fish. The section of river below Storm King is the center of striped bass spawning grounds. Every day, with each incoming and outgoing tide, fish would run a gauntlet past the uptake pipes. They predicted millions would be killed, destroying the commercial fishing industry (which of course was later shut down due to PCBs in 1977). But the argument was not, largely, a financial one; it was scenic and environmental. This was a first in judicial law, which set the path for future environmental litigation.

The battle was costly and complicated, and several times the environmental side lost, only to come back with better, clearer arguments, and stronger coalitions. Scenic Hudson formed during this period, as well as the Hudson River Fishermen's Association, led by Robert Boyle. When all of this settled, on December 19, 1980, for the first time in legal history the environment had rights. The mountain had the right to remain a mountain. This makes Storm King pretty special.

Truth is, Storm King is an ordinary mountain. It's a rounded hump with exposed granite on the south side, with a road like a gash across its belly. In Carl Carmer's book on the Hudson he mentions the mountain once, noting that the nineteenth-century writer Nathaniel Parker Willis wanted to change the name from Butter Hill to Storm King. Saving Butter Hill would have been much less compelling than saving Storm King.

The river *worn?* Storm King *ordinary?* These un-pious thoughts had roamed my mind since I had begun paddling the river; I never dared voice them. And then I met John. Despite a deep moral sense—his notions of right and wrong, the value of a promise and hard work unshakable—John is unsentimental about the river. "River shmiver!" he exclaimed during one of our conversations, sending me into gales of laughter. He is the environmentalist who has never hugged a tree. Didn't believe in hugging trees. And though I do hug trees, I found relief in John's perspective.

Near the cliffs of Storm King circled a kettle of turkey vultures, wings spread in a V. Their feathers fan out at the tips, as if they were fingers splayed out. They dipped around and around as if smelling an odorous carcass that would soon be a meal. From afar, the turkey vulture is an elegant, graceful bird. Up close it loses some of its appeal, particularly with its featherless red neck. What a vulture eats—often roadkill—is hard to think about. When alarmed, turkey vultures will vomit up their meals; the smell frightens off any predator.

The last time I had paddled this reach, I journeyed along the eastern shore. Now, sticking to the west, I was close to West Point. Young men jogged by on shore; on a trim grass field a soccer game was in play. The place looked peaceful, like a big summer camp. Once past World's End the real West Point emerges. The main building, Thayer

Hall, weds Gothic architecture with a medieval fortress and looks imposing. The building stands above the water, as if perched on the side of a cliff, and below a narrow strip of land leads to a dock.

The gap between West Point on the west and Constitution Island on the east side of the river is the narrowest section of the lower river. This is where patriots slung the chain to keep British boats from sailing further north. There's a section of that chain on Constitution Island. It's about two feet long and weighs 120 pounds. I find it hard to imagine that anyone thought it a good idea to put a chain across a river. Chains are heavy, and they sink. And this one did little to stop the British.

The land north of Con Hook is perhaps the prettiest I have seen anywhere on the river. It is sandy, with pine trees pressed flat by the wind. Rocks emerge from the sand. For the first time on the river, I felt that I knew this piece of land, though I'd never seen it before. I soon realized that it reminded me of the Indiana Dunes, where my family had summered with my grandparents. In an instant, I sensed the kiss of a breeze from the summer of 1971, when I was young and free, and my family was whole.

I understood why people go in search of their lost woods. This unexpected return to childhood brought with it as well all of the hope of childhood. In childhood, life is all about the future, looking to what will come next, what you will be "when you grow up." I needed a small taste of that hope.

Every day I was shocked by the emptiness of my life without my mother. Every morning, I hoped for an e-mail from her, or a phone call. When I visited my father in State College, I expected to arrive and find plans for dinner and a small bouquet of flowers next to my bed. Instead, the refrigerator was near-empty. The house, usually alive with smells and people, was spare. It was now seven months since my mother's death, and it felt still so fresh. For a month after her death, the sympathy poured in: cards, phone calls, walks in the woods to comfort me. All of that had trickled off, letting me know I was lingering too long in the loss.

I pushed out toward a green buoy, which marked the western boundary of the channel. As I started into the channel, I realized that an enormous barge was right behind me, chugging south. I had never seen anything so large moving on the river before, three barges lined up abreast, being pushed by one tug. Three barges wouldn't fit on my reach off Tivoli, and I realized how much wider and deeper, how much noisier and busier, the river was here.

I waited for the barges to pass, then I crossed the river and swung in near Mystery Point. I once visited the large house that stands at the point, when it was going to be a bed-and-breakfast. All of the bathrooms were done in marble with double showerheads. Scenic Hudson bought the surrounding land and house and then turned it over to Outward Bound to use as their main headquarters. The transformation of this house—from luxurious mansion to a base for land preservation and then to a home of outdoor education—followed the trail of Rose Hill and other houses in the valley. I wish it was as easy to transform a life.

Just south I landed on a spit at the tip of Manitou, a name that meant "Great Spirit" to the Algonquian-speaking tribes. These Indian place-names surface the length of the river, wedged between the Dutch Fishkill and Peekskill, the British Kingston and Hyde Park, the German Germantown and Rhinecliff. The Native Americans live on in Wappingers Falls, Esopus, Schodack, and Manhattan.

I grew up in the shadow of Nittany Mountain. A mural on the wall of the East Fairmont Elementary School cafeteria depicted the legend of Princess Nittany. When she died and was buried, the mountain rose from the earth, tomblike. I had hiked many times to the flat, sarcophagus-like summit of Mount Nittany, aware I was tromping on the resting spot of a princess. I hoped that schoolchildren in Wappingers Falls learned of the Wappinger tribes that gave their city its name.

I stood and stretched, tired after four hours of paddling. Within minutes John was there, full of energy, happy to have an excuse to be out on a brilliant day. While I organized gear, John wandered the narrow beach, distracted but focused at once. I looked over to see why he wasn't helping me with my gear and saw that he had come to a rest, as if he'd found what he was looking for. He stood with his back to a tree and lined up with a boxy white house on the far shore. He extended

his arms, fingers spread emphatically. I had no idea what he was pointing toward or looking at. At three in the afternoon, the sun-drilled
water flattened before me. Behind us, just twenty yards away, ran the
steel train tracks. South of us stretched the dozen houses of Manitou
that cling to the edge of the river.

"If you ever land here at high tide, line up with that house and this
tree, and you'll miss the rocks."

"OK," I said with little conviction. I hadn't spoken to anyone in
hours, and I'd slipped into a reverie on the river. "What's the story
with that house?" I gestured toward the nearest structure. Three stories
high, the plywood weathering black in the sun, it looked both clumsy
and desolate.

"See, if you line up you'll miss the rocks on either side." If I followed John's arm-directed trajectory I would land between rock out-
croppings, visible then at low tide, and onto the sandy shore. That was
where my kayak was beached.

"At high tide, you won't see those rocks."

"Right." But what he was suggesting was absurd. It had taken me
years to learn the details of tree limbs and rocks in my reach. The next
time I paddled this section of the Hudson I would not remember how
to line up for a scrape-free landing. To do so would require a memory
so expansive my mind bent imagining the possibility.

When Mark Twain was learning the Mississippi as a steamboat
pilot—a river four times the length of the Hudson and eight times
its navigable length—he balked at the supernatural memory required.
"Now, if my ears hear aright," he wrote, "I have not only to get the
names of all the towns and islands and bends and so on, by heart, but I
must even get up a warm personal acquaintanceship with every old snag
and one-limbed cotton-wood and obscure wood pile that ornaments
the banks of this river for twelve hundred miles; and more than that,
I must actually know where these things are in the dark." The problem
for Twain is my own in that "my memory was never loaded with anything
but blank cartridges." Twain is exaggerating, of course. But there was no
way that, day or night, I would recall the outlines of this landing.

I wished I knew the details of every landing along the Hudson
from Albany to Manhattan. I wanted to know who had landed and

what stories lived in the rocks that littered the shores. But the more I found out, the more there was to know, like those Russian dolls that keep emerging, one inside the other. *Learning a river is hard.*

Maybe that alone was worth learning.

John and I walked down the narrow road past several squat houses that all enjoyed small yards that edged the river. Several houses down, John stopped.

"This was my house."

It is a gray cape that looks like it belongs on Cape Cod. No cars sat in the driveway, so we walked around to the river's side of the house and peered in the window at the open living area, the cabinets he built, and the refrigerator that had fallen over on him. It was clear that he was heartbroken by returning to this place where he had lived for seventeen years. Here was a real home, where he saw the water go by, where he knew people by their boats. He suddenly, after three years, missed it horribly. There were many reasons to move, all of them related to being a good father and husband. I admired him for this, being able to sacrifice for those he loves. And I thought he was nuts to have let it go. *He had a house on the banks of the Hudson.*

John took me further down the train tracks to a piece of land that has remained undeveloped because there is no way to gain access. He used to take his daughter to this small cove when she was a child, and they would swim together. I imagined them floating for hours in this secret, rocky, shrub-strewn place. This river, this spot, was his world. And though he had sold the house, he could return here, to sit and watch the river go by. I envied that.

We walked back to John's car. I checked that my kayak was securely cinched to the roof rack, then scanned the rocky beach to be sure I had not left anything behind. The unfinished house caught my eye.

"What's the story with this house?" I still hadn't gotten an answer from him, and the house had to harbor good, nasty stories. But there's nothing sensational about its tale, other than the local zoning board. The owners claim it's but two stories high; it's clearly three. No one gave them a permit to build a three-story house, so midconstruction they abandoned the project. It looks odd in a stretch of the river where every inch of river shoreline is prized, where people buy homes for $700,000 and then tear them down to build new, more expensive ones.

This ordinary story I will remember, as well as the feel of the sun that day, the sweetness of the land near Con Hook, my panic in front of the *Virginia C.*, and John's sense of loss as he showed me the neat gray house where he used to live along the river there in Manitou.

13

IF YOU ARE LUCKY

Since my mother's death, images of her had appeared at odd, often inconvenient moments. As I stroked toward the abandoned railroad bridge north of Poughkeepsie, the picture I had was from the hour after she died. The nurses had straightened her blankets and applied a line of lipstick, which made her look poised after the hours of pain and struggle the night before. My father and I had held hands and stood next to her, while the sun filtered into her room. The memory brought tears that blurred my vision through my sunglasses. It was a gauzy day, the humidity high, so the tears mixed with sweat, mixed with the water of the river. I pulled my spray skirt back to let my legs breathe.

The afternoon sun swung in and out from behind thick dark clouds, mottling the river that sludged south. We had had days of heavy rain, and the effects were obvious. The water was an expansive mud puddle; debris bobbed about while branches and logs bunched together, creating loose rafts. I'd been paddling for three hours and had seen perhaps two motorboats. In a normally busy section of the river this emptiness made me uneasy. A white sheriff's boat zipped past, blue light spinning, interrupting my isolation.

I had put my boat in at eleven in the morning at Norrie Point, planning to take a snaky path south until I met up with John Cronin on his motorboat. He would then return me to Norrie. With a day before me, I felt full of hope as I paddled past motorboats patiently moored in the marina, and then a row of sailboats, hardware on the masts knocking as they rocked to the rhythm of wavelets. Clear of the boats, the river spread before me. On the far shore the former monastery Mount St. Alphonsus loomed majestic, a Romanesque castle above the river.

In the middle of the river, Esopus Island ballooned into view. The Canada geese Emmet and I had startled the year before had given up their posts. Perhaps they had already laid their eggs and the goslings had fledged. I ghosted by, admiring the slabs of rock that slip into the water. I soon passed the Poughkeepsie Yacht Club, sailboats gleaming in the sun. Just south and a hundred yards offshore, a miniature house shaped like a teepee squats on an island barely large enough to hold it. A small porch stares westward. I wanted to sit on that porch, but No Trespassing signs ring the islet.

On the smooth banks, daylilies bloomed, their deep orange illuminating the hillsides. The shoreline appears more natural on this stretch of the river, as the train tracks move inland. Here, the riprap that buttresses the shoreline is mercifully absent. I approached a stretch on the eastern shore known as Millionaire Mile, where the estates of the Vanderbilts and Roosevelts stand, tended by the National Park Service. Echoing them on the western shore in Ulster County is a series of convents and monasteries. Money on one side of the river, religion on the other side.

Though I find it a dull stretch of the river, it is a reach that has captured many travelers. Nathaniel Parker Willis writes: "The Hudson at Hyde Park is a broad, tranquil, and noble river, of about the same character as the Bosphorus above Roumeli-bissar, or the Dardanelles at Abydos. The shores are cultivated to the water's edge, and lean up in graceful, rather than bold elevations." Oliver Wendell Holmes described Willis as "an anticipation of Oscar Wilde," offering some insight into the excess here. But—the Bosphorus and the Dardanelles? It intrigues me that these straits are a point of comparison for the Hudson. The Hudson has been compared to many rivers, most often the Rhine by the many Palatine settlers in this region. This comparison inspired the names of the river communities of Rhinecliff and Rhinebeck. And those settlers were not mistaken. When I visited the Rhine, I saw that it was a broad, working river, just like the Hudson.

◊ ◊ ◊

A boat idling in the middle of the river looked like the usual fishing boat, but then out of the corner of my eye I saw three people haul in a fish that looked my size.

As I approached the flat-bottomed boat I could see it had a Department of Environmental Conservation logo on the side. Four DEC workers stood on board. A young man—he looked college age—turned and nodded hello. The other three, a woman and two men, remained focused on the fish lying still in front of them on a wooden platform that looked like a makeshift operating table. "We'll answer your questions in a moment," one of the state scientists said, scissors in hand.

"No rush," I said. I sidled up to a long net that hung at their side. In it lolled two more of the enormous fish. The top one was perhaps six feet long, torpedo-shaped, with a blunt snout. The exposed belly, white with pinkish tints, glinted near the surface of the water. *Sturgeon.*

I have a photo of a sturgeon on my bedroom wall; the Hudson River estuary logo, plastered throughout the valley, is a blue-colored sturgeon; I have heard sturgeon as they slap back into the river after one of their athletic vaults into the air. Photographs, images, sounds—I never imagined coming closer to a sturgeon. While no one watched, I reached out a hand and placed it on his exposed belly. I was touching a dinosaur.

Sturgeons are a relict species, that is, they haven't changed since the Mesozoic era, some 65–230 million years ago. So I was, in fact, touching something with a genetic code more ancient than the dinosaurs.

What did touching a sturgeon feel like? Smooth, like leather. Slick, like time. Solid, like love and death.

The young man who had initially greeted me scooped a hand into the water and rolled the fish over. On the flip side it was blue-black and scaleless; five rows of bony plates with sharp points called scutes ran down its long body.

"It weighs about 120," he said, without me asking.

My flesh and bones add up to the same.

The fish resumed its upside-down floating position, so that I could see its toothless oval underslung mouth; it opened and closed like a small animal searching, sightless, for a nipple. Four long white whiskers or barbells help it find food on the bottom of the river, which it siphons in through that elastic gaping mouth.

Because of their size, Atlantic sturgeon are described as monsters. They can grow to ten feet in length, and the heaviest have reached 800 pounds (though most weigh nearer 200). That they roam the bottom of the river gives them a touch of mystery; those scutes make them appear tough. Despite all this, there was a sweetness to this fish I never could have imagined. It was not its helplessness, but rather a gentleness, apparent in that mouth, gumming the air.

"It's OK?" I asked.

"It's fine," he assured me, though I wasn't comforted. No captured animal is fine. And sturgeons under stress float upside down, as this one did.

On the boat, the woman held a hose that led from the river up to the fish they were operating on. This kept water flowing through its gills. The two men worked silently, splotches of blood evident on their hands.

"We're tagging the sturgeon," the one explained. They were placing four different tags in or on this fish, including one with satellite contact to track its movements. The two fish in the net awaited their tags.

"We don't know where they go once they leave the Hudson," he explained. Sturgeon are loyal to the river, returning from the ocean to spawn in freshwater where they were born. Scientists have been able to study the sturgeon in the river, so they know when they begin to mate (at nine to twenty-three years old, but the average age of reproduction is twelve), how many eggs are produced (two million), and how long the young stay in freshwater before heading to sea (two to seven years). After that little is known.

Studying the movement of sturgeon will help to preserve the fish. Scientists want to have a better sense of how sturgeon return to their river of origin. Then they can determine if farm-hatched fish can successfully move through their life cycle. Results of the study are still in progress, but here is one finding: "When all sonic tagged sturgeon locations were examined, they were found most often in dynamic mud." *Dynamic mud.* I've never questioned that scientists are poets in disguise, and I can imagine the jolt of delight when they came up with this near oxymoron. There was, though, nothing near to dynamic about the fish in front of me.

Sturgeon are rare. There are twenty-six species of sturgeon found throughout the Northern Hemisphere, and all have been overfished. Two species, the Atlantic and the shortnose, live in the Hudson. Since 1967 the shortnose has been classified endangered. Yet it turns out the river is good to them: the largest shortnose populations have been counted in the Hudson. The Atlantic is protected in the river and along the coast, where commercial fishermen once intercepted sturgeon before they could reach the river to spawn.

In the nineteenth and early twentieth centuries sturgeon were so common in the Hudson they were referred to as Albany beef. But what sturgeon are most prized for are their eggs, which, when unfertilized, are made into caviar. The golden-brown eggs of the Hudson River sturgeon rank up there with beluga. In one of his most engaging chapters in *The Hudson*, Robert Boyle describes the legendary sturgeon fisherman Ace Lent. Big and taciturn, he often worked with his cousin Spitz. (I love these names; in fact, it seems that to be a commercial fisherman on the river you had to have such a name: Turk DeGroat, Tucker Crawford, Everett Nack, Gussie Zahn, Henry Gourdine.) Because Ace Lent could pull sturgeon out of the river so easily, Boyle schemed to start the Greater Verplanck Caviar Company. He describes the glee of imagining all the caviar—and money. But, like many great ideas, this one faltered for lack of funding before it started.

A fish that begins to mate so late in life is hard to bring back. But the ban on fishing and a cleaner river mean that the sturgeon is in fact returning. These scientists had easily snagged these three sturgeon with gill nets. They explained that this was sturgeon mating ground and this was their mating season.

"Where'd you buy your kayak?" the young man on the boat asked.

There was nothing special about my kayak, but I could see by his eager expression that he would have preferred to be out paddling. I wanted to say, *Let's swap places.* I will stand there and memorize the belly of the fish, the curves and lines of grace and tenacity. I will stand there and dream of the past and imagine the future.

I did not want to leave. I wanted to see the sturgeon lift from the table and swim free, but I knew it would be hours before it recovered from the anesthetic. I remembered my mother (one foot shorter and twenty pounds lighter than the sturgeon) hours after surgery, a groggy smile letting me know she was but halfway returned to this world. I gave her juice from a sip cup and held her hand. Who would tend the sturgeon in recovery?

I pointed south, after bidding the sturgeon and the DEC staff farewell. I passed Bard Rock, which sticks into the river from the Vanderbilt property. Soon, the bulky cream-colored mansion emerged through the tops of the trees. At the mouth of Crum Elbow Creek a few boats lazed in the water. I pushed on, feeling that around the bend rested the next wondrous sight. The sturgeon left me wanting more of the magic from the river.

Once I passed Rogers Point (unfortunately not named after a relative), with a line of motorboats moored at a private wooden dock that frames the river, I settled into a meditative stroke, the current working with me. This was the section Robert Juet had named the Lange Rack, or Long Reach. I could see long into the distance, to hills on the western horizon. If I swung around in my boat, facing west and north, the Catskills appeared close by.

As if to prepare travelers for the industry of Poughkeepsie, the train tracks reemerged close to shore, on both sides of the river, squeezing the river in, narrow and straight. Freight trains, which move north and south on the western shore, usually run inland. But in certain stretches they nudge the river. Often over one hundred cars long, they clank by less frequently and more slowly than passenger trains on the eastern shore.

I passed the Culinary Institute of America (known to locals as the CIA) with its solid brick buildings. These buildings, originally a mansion, became a Jesuit monastery, St. Andrew-on-Hudson, before becoming a culinary school. The priest and paleontologist Pierre Teilhard de Chardin is buried there, though he is not the patron saint of chefs. He spent his life writing about Christian theology and evolution but never saw his masterwork, *The Phenomenon of Man*, in print. The church suppressed his Hegelian and Darwinian ideas on how consciousness is evolving toward what he called the Omega Point. The earth itself was developing an organ of consciousness, the *noosphere*. (In my mind, this invention of language makes Teilhard de Chardin a dynamic mud person.) Would he have taken pleasure in touching a sturgeon, a creature so sure of itself, so complete in design, it had shrugged off millennia of biological and ecological change?

Marist College has property that runs to the river's edge, and several high-rise dorms look out on the river. The college's docks line the water. On the western shore messy graffiti marked the beautiful long slabs of rock that descend to the railroad tracks. One message, 99, covered over a previous illegible blur of white paint. A large *L* (for *Love?*) on one rock and a grand *R* (for the Marist Red Foxes?) appeared faintly. A young man in a scull swooshed past me going north with amazing grace, then after a pause again passed me on his course to the south.

The sheriff's boat that had passed me earlier hovered in the water just ahead and under the abandoned steel railroad bridge, its blue light twirling. The wooden decking of the steel bridge burned in 1974, and since then the bridge had undergone a slow decline. Some wanted to tear it down, and others wanted to make it into a pedestrian bridge that would connect Poughkeepsie and Highland. News was that the latter group had won, and the bridge would open in 2009. On the eastern shore, several officers stood in their crisp blue uniforms, and I imagined they were apprehending a homeless man who had set up an encampment there in the seclusion of rock, concrete, and unruly shrubs by the side of the river.

And then I saw it, or him, a human body. What could be more familiar? But this body was spread eagle on a slab of concrete, a male figure, larger than human, bloated and a violent purple-black color. I couldn't understand what I was seeing, or rather, I knew what lay there was a dead body, but it just didn't quite make sense. This, like the sturgeon, was something I expected in movies or photographs. I knew that people drowned in the river several times a year; I read articles in the local papers about people jumping from bridges. But I never thought I'd be there to see a body washed up on shore. I looked briefly, confirming what I saw, but not wanting the image to become imbedded in my mind. I noted the blue-jean shorts, the tan work boots, but I don't know what kind of shirt he wore or the color of his hair. I just remember his distorted shape, limp and oversized, as if the body had been inflated.

For a while this body would be just a body—without a name, a home, a family and friends. Who had loved this man? It is love that transforms a body into a person, gives him a past, a place in the world.

The officers on shore stood at a good distance, hovering near the tall grasses and weeds that encircled the hard resting spot of the dead man. They talked amongst themselves, and I imagined their own reticence to be near or to touch the dead. Meanwhile, the corpse warmed in the summer sun. I stopped for a moment, hovering in the water to catch my breath. I covered my mouth to keep the tears from emerging and shook my head to erase the images that moved from the bloated body on shore to my mother in her peacefulness.

Then I continued to paddle south—what else could I do?

I passed the sheriff's boat and shook my head, an odd gesture of commiseration. And then I really started to cry. Not for this stranger whose story I didn't know, but for thinking of death, of my stilled mother as my father and I came into her room before dawn on the morning that she died. I pictured wrestling her rose-cut diamond ring from her finger, the gesture practical but also intimate. My father kissed her forehead, her lips, told her that he loved her. I placed a hand on her body, touched the soft flesh covering her limp frame, and kissed her cold gentle cheek, a final good-bye. What else could I do?

I couldn't pass through Poughkeepsie fast enough. It was loud. The noise from the Mid-Hudson Bridge, and the blur of traffic down Route 9, mixed with the crank of machinery on the shoreline, both construction and industry. An Amtrak train whistled as it announced its arrival at the station.

Forty-five minutes later, I was emerging from that mess, the shoreline on the western side returning to trees and leafy bushes, and the blight of the eastern shore thinning, when I spied John's boat, obvious from a distance with its tower rising high in the air. He saw me as well—his boat turned toward me—and within minutes he was idling in the water a few feet away. It's a beautiful boat, twenty-nine feet long with hardwood floors. The stern, painted a deep green, displays the name *Trust*. John stood at the stern and smiled down on me. He looked like summer, his ginger-colored hair disheveled by the wind. I could not have been happier to see someone.

"I'm completely undone," I said. "There's a dead body just up the river."

"That's the river," he said. "In my years I've seen two."

His casualness took a bit of the edge off of my feeling that I'd been to the end of the world and back. I hauled my kayak on deck and settled in with an ice-cold soda water.

John explained that he was late leaving Beacon, as when he set out he met a gaggle of boys launching a makeshift raft.

"They were headed for Manhattan."

Marvelous, I thought.

"They didn't have any water," he said. "I had to go buy them water."

I smiled at John's affectionate frustration. What would the river be like if teenage boys didn't want to head out on a raft with hope and no water?

"We'll be reading about them in the papers in two days."

We began our journey north. The wind in my ears felt easy as we moved back into Poughkeepsie, back toward the dead man. Just as I began to relax with the movement of the boat, the engine made an odd whirring sound, and the oil alarm rang a high-pitched squeal. John shut off the engine and called his mechanic, who knows the

boat inside and out. John checked various pressures and oil levels as
we straddled the middle of the river. There's no reason to drag out the
long minutes of questioning and testing; the boat was going nowhere.
The same sheriff I'd seen by the bridge appeared and asked if we
wanted a tow.

"Don't you have anything else to do?" John joked.

"No, just pulled a body out of the river."

"So I heard. Was he a jumper?"

A jumper.

The sheriff threw us a rope and towed us south for three miles to
White's Marina, a busy dock in New Hamburg. Once on the dock, I
thanked the sheriff.

"I thought that was you in the kayak. I thought you didn't see
the body. Then it was clear you had." So they had been watching me,
anticipating my reaction, that moment when I stopped paddling and
covered my mouth, the gesture of surprise, of horror, of holding back
tears.

"It was a difficult sight," I said.

"You should have seen when they turned it over."

It.

They had been looking for his body for four days. He'd leapt off
the dock late at night in Poughkeepsie.

"He had deformed arms," the sheriff explained, making one hand
into a blade that cut at his strong, tanned elbows.

"So he didn't intend to swim?"

He nodded.

A jumper, but not from a bridge. The next day the *Poughkeepsie Journal* listed the cause of death as drowning.

"Does this happen often?" I asked.

"A few every summer." The sheriff, practical and honest, betrayed
a hint of sadness.

While John tended to the details of the silenced *Trust*, I walked
around the marina, admiring boats. The busyness of a dock so late in
the day surprised me. Men just off from work slipped out for a few
moments of freedom on the water. Fathers yelled at their sons as they
maneuvered their ungainly, precious boats into the water. Soon, the

sun started its inevitable arc toward the west. I sat on the wooden dock savoring the smells of creosote and engine oil, and looked west at the limestone cliffs on the far shore.

A few every summer.

This is what I understood as I sat and watched the sun disappear. If you are on the river long enough, a death is inevitable, something you will see. If you are on the river long enough, you will meet a sturgeon. If you are lucky, you will get to touch it. And if you live long enough, you will see someone you love die. If you are lucky, you will get to kiss her good-bye.

14

FISHING

"Catch anything?"

My voice sounded too loud, interrupting the silent space between water and shoreline. I swung out to avoid the pellucid lines that reflect a faint glimmer before vanishing into the dark. I like to leave fishermen as much space as possible, as they have an invisible but palpable zone marked off asking for quiet, asking for people to keep away.

The fishermen stand without slouching at river's edge or else they perch on coolers, surveying the several lines they've cast that stretch taut from land to water. Some have a son in tow—fidgeting, casting, and reeling, not yet having learned the art of patience. Some start small fires to keep warm, and the smell of wood smoke drifts onto the river.

When I first began paddling, I had the notion that fishermen and I would share a rare bond, that though I am not a fisherwoman, we are kin of sorts. Together, miles from the nearest town, we would share the glee of our isolation, and they would welcome me into the brotherhood of solitude. We'd celebrate the day, and I'd float while we swapped sightings. I even imagined I could give them tips, tell them about those places I'd seen fish leap into the air, then slap back into the water. In exchange, they might offer, in a few quick words, a snippet of wisdom. Surely, after years of returning to the banks of the Hudson, of timing their lives to the concealed movement of striped bass, they must know secrets about the river. And about life. I romanticize these fishermen even though I know that most of them are simply men with time and a pole and a desire to stand near the Hudson River.

"What are you fishing for?" I sometimes ask.

I imagine they are fishing for striped bass, as they are legendary in these waters. Fishermen come in fast boats from all over the country for the bass-fishing competitions.

"I don't know," one fisherman answered. Many respond, "Whatever."

Over 200 species of fish have been recorded in the Hudson River basin, so "whatever" could mean reeling in an eel or white perch, a sunfish, carp, or bluefish.

I wonder how many eat what they catch. Fish, like turtles, are contaminated by PCBs. In 1975 a vibrant commercial fishing industry was shut down because of the toxins. Commercial fishermen continued their trade in shad and crab because these enter the estuary to spawn but spend their lives in open water. These fishermen were but a handful, where there used to be hundreds jockeying for the prime spots. PCBs changed the life of the Hudson. Now, shad fishing has also been shut down, ending an era of Hudson River fishing. This move is lamented by some—a trade, a tradition, a way of life is gone—but it is celebrated by those who want to save a fish. "Logging old growth trees is a tradition too," John Lipscomb told me to make his point.

Yet where there is a river, people will fish. And regardless of warnings, people will eat their catch—a maximum of one striped bass a month is recommended. But there are few of these brave or incautious fishermen who time their lives to movement of fish.

"Catch anything?"

"Nothing yet."

Nothing yet. Hope remains in the response. There's yet time to catch a fish, perhaps proof of a fisherman's intangible pursuits.

◊ ◊ ◊

I have not fished on the Hudson, and have had but one fishing experience.

I was twelve when my aunt, uncle, and cousin Andrew, whom we then called Andy, took me with them to Eagle's Nest, their island in Trafalgar Bay in the Boundary Waters of Canada. My journal from that week in the wild is filled with accounts of swimming, floating on an inner tube, building a tree fort, picking blueberries "bigger than ones found in the grocery store," playing games of hearts (scores recorded; I lost pretty consistently), and fishing. I got up near dawn to fish alone. In the afternoons Andy and I trolled around the island in a canoe. There are many lost lures and some disappointment; from time to time Andy or his father, Ray, caught a fish. My eagerness to catch a fish remains a vital memory, even though Andy and I ate sloppy joes and applesauce the night Aunt Mary Louise and Uncle Ray ate their fresh catch. The thrill of fishing was irresistible, and when we found a sweet spot—a shelf at the end of the island—Andy and I returned there every day. While the pursuit was fun, I worried what would happen if I actually caught a fish—I would have to kill, and clean it. When Ray had taught his son how to clean a fish, I watched at a distance.

On my final day on the island, Ray took me out in the metal canoe for a last try. It was dusk, and it was calm on the lake. After an hour or so, dinner called us back to the cabin. Ray encouraged me to troll, though I had fallen into a glum disappointment. Ray insisted I drop my line in the water, so I rallied, if only to please him.

Almost home, I sensed a snag, and Ray back paddled. Then the jerk at the end of my line told me I had what I'd been waiting for. My young journal entry reads: "IT WAS A FISH!!!!!" And the day concludes: "After Ray cleaned *my* fish we played Oh Hell. Then we all went to bed. This has been my best day at the island."

I can still feel the wrestle of bringing that trout into the canoe, my arms strained, convinced it had to weigh twenty pounds or more. That lake trout lies at the heart of that trip, the central event, or rather the event the entire trip led up to. The trout would never have been caught without my uncle, who opened a new door of outdoor pleasure for me. But what Ray really taught me was about writing.

I kept my journal hidden under the mattress of the bunk bed where I slept. At the beginning of my journal I wrote: "STOP. This is my personnal [*sic*] diary of my feelings *please* do not look." I lived in fear of someone reading what I wrote. As an adult I still keep a daily journal, and I still worry about people reading it. But that doesn't stop me from writing, because what I feel when I write is rare, something found in isolated places, say, in a kayak or on a riverbank. Writer, kayaker, or fisherman—in the sheltered place of words or of gestures, a person can be herself. That is why I was upset when Ray told me that he had read my journal.

In writing a journal everyone imagines an audience. Or even hopes for an audience—if someone cares to read about my daily life, emotions, and thoughts, then the stories of my life must be worth reading, must be, even, important. For me, like most little girls, that audience was my father. I imagined him a curious but critical reader. But on this trip I had imagined Ray as my reader, noting the things I knew he would find important to chronicle: the number of blueberries in each pancake, a sign of how many blueberries we had picked; or a long description of how we had built our tree house. I wanted him to admire my observations as much as he had admired the way I swung high on the tree swing, landing with a plop into the deep waters of the lake.

I wonder for the fishermen who their audience is—the people at home who will admire the fish they've caught or the photos where they grin, holding their catch? Or perhaps it is whoever will listen to the tales they tell of the big one that got away? The fishermen and I share this love of the good story. But the real story, the act of fishing or writing, is private.

◊ ◊ ◊

Years later Ray gave Becky and me a book, titled *Small Voices,* a selection from the diaries of children under the age of thirteen. He inscribed the book: *To Becky and Susie with love from their favorite uncle. P.S. I know it's hard, with such a father as you have, to keep writing—but some of these kids had such obstacles, too.*

Having a father who is a writer is an obstacle. The obstacle is that he did not want me to be a writer. He wanted me to be a happy girl, and he knew that writing and happiness are not easily twinned. So when I took to writing in college he despaired. He wished I had picked something—anything—more of this world, something that wouldn't isolate me and make me a bit goofy, the way he had become.

Having a writer as a father also is an asset. I grew up around books and words. Books mattered. My grandfather never quite understood what my father did until the day he sold his first novel to the movies. That money made my father's work real. When I said I wanted to write, my father got it. I didn't need to explain anything, not why I wanted to do it or what it meant to be a writer. And he knew too well the struggle ahead of me, and that from time to time it would also be pure pleasure.

Ray believed in trolling one last time that final evening on the island. I can still hear his words of encouragement beating inside of me. Ray taught me about persistence, or, rather, hope. Fishing and writing are about hope. The odds are not good that you'll find a fish or that you'll find the right word. But from time to time you do.

15

CIRCLING THE CITY

I am drawn to the edges—of cliffs, of rivers—to the places of beginnings and endings. So it wasn't long before I was pulled south—to Manhattan, where the Hudson joins the Atlantic Ocean. Because it is so different from my peaceful reach and because I could not claim to know the Hudson if I had not paddled the stretch that licks the western side of Manhattan, I wanted to circumnavigate the city.

If New York City holds a mythological status—for both its glory and its seedier qualities—so too do the waters that flow around the city. It is a challenge that kayakers revel in. The Manhattan Kayak Company advertises the tour in this way: "O.K., ready for the big one? Welcome to a 2,000 calorie fueled circle line style tour of Manhattan. Don't tell us we didn't warn you—this one is hard." It is hard—the hardest paddle you can find on the Hudson River.

It is often the gruesome side of the venture that people focus on. Stories of dead bodies, called floaters, abound. More common are dead rats or fish, bloated and bobbing in the surf. When swimmers jump in they usually opt for a tetanus shot. It is a good idea. There are fourteen wastewater treatment plants in and around the city, discharging 1.4 billion gallons of treated water every day. Add to this a stream of boats—ferries, water taxis, pleasure boats, tankers, tugs with barges, freighters, oceangoing passenger ships, tour boats—and the tricky currents, and you have by far the most complicated and dangerous waters on the Hudson.

The summer of 2005, when my mother was limping through chemotherapy, my friend Dawes Strickler called on a Saturday afternoon. "Want to paddle Manhattan tomorrow?" he asked. He had planned to go alone, but his wife was threatening divorce if he didn't find someone to go with him.

"You know how to self-rescue, right?" Dawes asked.

"Sure," I said with confidence. But I had never had to test those skills, especially not in the wake of the Staten Island Ferry.

I have to admit that, blinded by hours of fear, I remember almost nothing except the beginning and the end of the trip. I had left home at 2:00 a.m. By 5:30 we had parked in New Jersey and pushed off from Liberty State Park. Crossing the expansive New York Harbor, the sun in our eyes, the Statue of Liberty waving at our side, I had felt tiny yet strong.

The trip had gone well up the East River, through Hell Gate and onto the Harlem River, then back onto the Hudson. There, cruising the middle of the river at seven knots (Dawes had a GPS and regularly announced our speed), I felt victorious. And then an ocean wind emerged from the south. Because the wind ran counter to the current, which was at full ebb, waves with white caps knocked me around. My already weary arms were near collapse as we neared the end of our thirty-four miles. We crossed the river, back toward New Jersey. Seeking the comfort of land, I hugged in near the rock wall that supports Ellis Island. Out of nowhere a Coast Guard boat emerged, rocking me more violently in the tumultuous water. They were not coming to help me; they wanted identification. I could not let go of my paddle long enough to hand over ID, so they followed us for forty-five minutes into a bay out of the wind. There they handed us each a $50 fine for "violating a security zone."

Certainly everyone must be able to see the difference between a middle-aged woman clutching her paddle and trying not to capsize and someone intent on terrorist acts. The only thing I could deploy that afternoon was a cloud of frustration.

After that long day of paddling I might have been satisfied, like a person who completes the New York City Marathon hangs up her shoes and lives off of that glory for years. I had my good story. But for some reason I had to come back. My motivations were unclear. What I did know was that for nine hours all I would think about was the next stroke, whether I had to avoid a boat, or where we might stop for a brief, smelly rest. These tours required concentration and commitment; I had to be focused in mind and body. If I had needed the distraction and rush of New York's waters in 2005, now, in the wake of my mother's death, I needed it even more.

◊ ◊ ◊

I met Dawes and a woman I know as Military Sue near West Point, where they both work, and together we drove south. I confessed I had not slept. Dawes admitted he had not either.

"I slept fine," Sue said, which meant she had no idea what she was getting into.

This year we were launching out of Englewood, New Jersey. Englewood is right under the Palisades, those dramatic reddish-colored cliffs that rise as high as 550 feet and run for 20 miles, framing the west side of the river. The Lenape, who lived along the banks of the lower west side of the river, called the cliffs "rocks that look like rows of trees." It is here, in its final 21.9 miles that the Hudson is shared with another state, New Jersey. Otherwise, its journey from source to ocean is in New York State.

We were ready to go at 12:30. Sue waded out through the thick muck of low tide, steadied the boat Dawes had borrowed for her, and then entered it as if executing a gymnastic routine. "How do I hold the paddle?" she asked. *Oh dear*, I thought. I knew she had little experience, but it was news to she had none. Yet Sue has the virtues of strength and will. She is a rock climber, and climbers believe they can do anything, including defy gravity. But this was like asking someone who has never once jogged to run a marathon.

Dawes teaches rock climbing at West Point, and he looks the part: short blond hair, a solid jaw, strong all around. He laughs easily and loves the natural world. He had done this paddle for the past six years, so I knew that he could be trusted to plan out our trip, matching our movement to the currents. Every year he brought someone new, whom he nurtured through the day. I was the only person to return for another round. Yet before launching, my body was almost toxic with adrenalin. The jouncy feeling that gave me was both familiar and fun.

"That's where we'll come out," Dawes said, pointing to Spuyten Duyvil on the eastern shore. It seemed so far away, not just because it was a mile across, but because between now and when we would emerge there were at least eight hours of paddling.

I watched Sue teeter in her boat. The great advantage of having Sue along was I had someone to worry about beside myself. We gave her a two-minute paddle instruction—brace your legs inside the boat for stability and leverage, keep your elbows low, and use your torso to paddle—and we were off down the Hudson. Right down the middle, to be exact, so we could catch the last of the current.

Both shores vanished as we glided under the George Washington Bridge, which, viewed from the water, allowed us to thrill in the towers soaring 604 feet overhead. The sun glinted off of the steel beams, the sky nearly cloudless. South of the bridge, I coasted closer to the Manhattan shoreline, so the western shore of New Jersey was but a blur to my right. Dawes stuck further out in the river, with Sue tagging close behind him.

As we passed the stone tower of Riverside Church at 121st Street, the wind emerged from the south. Since the wind was moving counter to the current, an erratic chop formed that made me feel like a drunken duck, bobbing from one wave to the next. I assumed Sue had to be terrified. But there she was shoveling through the water, her straw hat perched on her head, exclaiming, "I love this!"

We struggled with the wind for the length of the city. The wind carried the smell of the ocean, a wet, salt mix that spoke of big waves and deep waters. Both invigorating and exhausting, the wind kept my attention focused on forward movement. I was interested in what was on shore only in order to gauge my progress. The first marker that held meaning for me was the Seventy-ninth Street Boat Basin, where a few people live year-round in their boats.

When I lived in Manhattan, I bicycled from my apartment at 159th Street and Riverside Drive to my office at Fiftieth and Broadway. Sticking to Riverside Park made this a graceful morning commute, except for the final stretch, inhaling bus fumes on Broadway. After work I would bicycle to a wall just south of the Seventy-ninth Street Boat Basin. The wall supported the West Side Highway—the clank of traffic overhead never stopped—and below the wall a grate kept me from plummeting over a hundred feet into a mysterious abyss. A sign warned, "Do not walk on grate."

I traversed back and forth on that wall, keeping my fingers and forearms in shape for climbing. From time to time I would fall, landing hard on the grate. I'd chalk up my hands and step back onto the wall, all of the sharp holds coated with a thin dust. Once my arms were exhausted, I would coast down to the marina at Seventy-ninth Street and look at the sailboats, and motorboats, many of which looked like they were docked for the duration of their lives. Other than those moments, I paid little attention to the river that now ran through my life.

The river that wraps the western edge of Manhattan felt familiar to me. It was related to the waters further north that I knew well. As on my reach, the river expanded my sense of space. There was the same open sky, and the long views to the distance. The difference I felt is that here the waters run deeper, between fifty and sixty feet, and just around the bend rolls the Atlantic Ocean. The smell of the water was not that of urban myth, but the same rich mixture of oil, natural decay, and freedom that I know so well. The biggest difference was the sense I had of the mass of life just off my left shoulder. I could feel that energy radiating out onto the water, pushing me forward. I did not let up to admire a skyscraper, a riverside restaurant, or to engage thoughts of loss. I pushed forward, stroke after stroke.

Starting at Fifty-ninth Street, long docks jut into the river, and we gave them and their traffic a safe berth. The unmistakable World War II aircraft carrier, *Intrepid*, sat still at dock. Except for such obvious sights, the city was far away, a faint hum of traffic, a glitter of steel and glass. Out on the river, the sun bathed us while clouds ran loose across the sky. As we neared the end of the island, I thought of the twin towers that should have greeted us.

At the Battery I called out to Dawes, ahead of us both, "Let's stick together."

The lower end of Manhattan made me nervous, as boat traffic becomes thick with water taxis (which move with the same fanatic energy as real taxis), ferries, the Circle Line tour boats, and the enormous orange Staten Island Ferry. "Think of a chipmunk crossing three lanes of traffic. We're the chipmunks," Dawes explained to Sue as we hovered for a moment to regroup.

Though small boats often have the right-of-way, that is not the reality in these waters. Here, the unwritten "rule of tonnage" applied—if a boat is bigger than you, it has the right-of-way. The New York State Parks Department spells out these rules, derived from Coast Guard guidelines:

    I. When two vessels are on a collision course in a crossing situation, the vessel on the right has the right of way.

    II. Vessels without mechanized power have the right of way; but smaller vessels must yield to larger vessels that do not have the same maneuverability. These include sludge carrying ships, oil tankers and barges and any large commercial vessel. It is also wise to yield to fast-moving motorboats. A vessel being overtaken should maintain its speed and direction.

    III. A vessel overtaking another should stay clear of the craft being overtaken.

    IV. In any case, take whatever action is necessary to avoid the collision.

In any case it is wise to know that even if you do have the right-of-way, don't act like you do. Here's a little something from sailors warning of what happens if you insist on your right-of-way:

> *Here lies the body of Danny O'Day*
> *Who died defending his right of way*
> *He was right, dead right, as the day is long*
> *But he's just as dead as if he'd been wrong*

It's a good little ditty to memorize.

The greatest menace was not, in fact, the water taxis, which, though speedy, have a regular come-and-go and sober, licensed pilots. It was the few rogue pleasure boats that appeared out of nowhere that frightened me. We'd call out, "Coming at us; no, turning; no, coming at us!" They'd careen past, churning up large wakes. If those wakes struck us head-on, our boats would rise and slap back down into the water. If they came from behind, the waves would lift and carry us, and we would surf. If they smacked us on our port or starboard sides the belly of the boat lifted, and if we didn't adjust our weight with our hips, or brace with our paddles to stabilize, there was an unsettling sense of toppling over.

When we rounded the Battery, life calmed a bit. "If you can do that you can do anything," I told Sue, impressed she'd made it through the maze of waves and boats.

After three and a half hours on the water, arms tired, and lower back tense from sitting, we were ready for a break. We hugged the edge of Lower Manhattan, then coasted to a stop on a slim, sandy beach exposed at low tide, under the Brooklyn Bridge. Four feet wide and strewn with plastic bottles, this beach seemed a hidden gem—until we saw and smelled an engorged, hairless rat, splayed out on the sand, its little paws open to the sky. The smell of rotting rat pushed us to the edge of our landing. The din of traffic on the Brooklyn Bridge rattled down to the beach as Dawes pointed out the cement supports for the bridge, made from limestone taken from the hills near Rosendale. It's tough natural cement: 136 years after the beginning of the bridge's construction there was no visible decay.

I had often walked or bicycled across the Brooklyn Bridge, which was crowded on weekends and at rush hour with commuters walking to and from work. Walking the 1,595.5 feet brought the two boroughs together. The view from the water was different; I could make out the Brooklyn waterfront, but with little detail. Brooklyn was the far shore and far away. Our world shrunk to the small beach where we had landed.

The beach was separated from a sidewalk by a waist-high chain-link fence. People stopped and stared at us; one elderly couple asked questions about what we had done and where we were going; and Sue and I wondered where we were going to pee.

I pulled out hand wipes and offered one to Sue and Dawes. "It's too late," Sue said, taking a handful of gorp. I figured eating with water-soaked hands would be like eating after rubbing my palms on the sidewalk at Broadway and Seventy-ninth. I wiped my hands clean, realizing that this was but a small gesture—I'd already tasted plenty of salt water that had sprayed onto my face.

While I ate the first of my peanut-butter sandwiches, washed down with lukewarm water, Sue wandered off, leaned against the cement breakwater, slipped down her shorts, and peed. When she returned I nodded to the two men sitting on the bench above where she had squatted.

"I didn't realize they were there," she laughed.

"What could they see?" I shrugged, and followed her lead.

"Are we halfway?" Sue asked.

Dawes and I looked at each other. "Almost," we said in unison. And we knew we were lying. What lay ahead was half the trip, but the waters we were entering were tricky, the currents complicated. We thought we had the timing down, but the final section above Hell Gate had, in the past, surprised Dawes and other paddlers with unlikely currents. It could be hard.

"I'm not sure I can make it."

I had watched Sue paddle, and though she kept reporting, "I think I got it"—and she was making extraordinary progress—somehow our "Keep your elbows low" directive hadn't sunk in. Her shoulders ached. There were few options short of Sue waiting for hours for us to retrieve her. And in that time the beach would vanish with the high tide. We didn't need to voice this, and we didn't discuss options; in ten minutes we all busied ourselves repacking our boats.

The East River where it falls into New York Harbor is wide. Boat traffic in this lower part of the river was thick. So we once again grouped together and moved midstream, away from the docks. At this point we had a strong current with us, and a slight wind at our backs. We moved quickly, and as traffic thinned, were able to appreciate the astonishing views of the city on this clear day. With no humidity, the buildings cut a neat line, glass windows shimmering.

On the East River, I was on an unfamiliar river. Or rather, a strait, as the East River connects New York Bay with Long Island Sound. The current, responding to the narrow passage of the strait, ran deep and powerfully below my boat. There were sections where a sewage-like smell rose from the water. I no longer had the open sky of the Hudson River as the skyline of Manhattan shadowed my view.

Despite the fact I was not in familiar waters, because of my water-line perspective, I felt close to the city. In my reach, I often become dreamy as I bob near snapping turtles and cattails. Nature is at my elbow. In this urban setting, though, I was developing a relationship with steel, concrete, and brown-green water. Paddling up the East River was like entering a house through the back door. The docks appeared worn. Just beyond the docks, tall buildings glittered in the summer light.

Just off the United Nations Headquarters, located on the East River Drive between Forty-second and Forty-eighth streets in the Turtle Bay neighborhood, is a small outcropping, which is a pile of dredge. On it, double-crested cormorants draped their wings to dry. On the island a sign reads U Thant Island, for the Burmese Buddhist Secretary-General of the United Nations, U Thant. And the arch on which the cormorants rested is a Peace Arch. In fact, the island isn't named U Thant, it's named Belmont, for the industrialist who built one of the thirteen tunnels that burrow under the East River. The debris removed to build one of those tunnels was heaped on a reef, so there stands this unnatural island. It is but one of many man-made features in the East River. The shoreline has been extended with landfill; islands have merged and emerged from dredging. Dredging, blasting, filling—we have altered this waterway.

And yet the natural world was never far away. No one paddles around Manhattan for the nature sightings, but when I saw something—the jellyfish floating in the water (though later I learned they are a nuisance, and a sign of pollution), the glorious egret and several blue heron taking flight—I felt a surge of excitement.

Roosevelt Island, a two-mile-long thin island, fills the river between Manhattan and Queens. We took to the western side, passing under the Queensboro Bridge. At the northern tip of Roosevelt Island we were entering the interesting section called Hell Gate. If we swung to the east we would have passed under the Triborough Bridge (now the Robert F. Kennedy Bridge), but we stayed west, toward the island called Mill Rock and into the Harlem River.

Something about the name Hell Gate makes it seem as if it should be treacherous, and historically these waters were—many ships sunk near there in the nineteenth century. But the original Dutch name, Hellegat, means "bright passage" (that is, one interpretation says this; others offer that Hell Gate means "hell channel"). For us—and for most who pass through this section—it was a bright passage. At the end of the nineteenth century the Army Corps of Engineers blasted the rocks and reefs that once made the passing dangerous. Still, Hell Gate remains tricky, as the tide-driven currents from New York Harbor, the Harlem River, and Long Island Sound converge. It was crucial that we had hit it near slack tide. Dawes had timed our paddle with precision.

Eight bridges span the East River, and each has its own personality: high or low, arched or more flat, steel or cement supports. Those bridges became my markers, the points I aimed for, each one signaling that I had completed one more lap toward the end. Paddling under the bridges, I took in the thunder of traffic overhead. All of the bridges clank and rattle with cars and trucks, except for a blue-green pedestrian bridge that traverses from Manhattan to Wards Island. On the island is a state mental hospital, surrounded by wire fencing; tiny windows look out onto the river.

On the East River we flew along—faster at times than cars jam-packed on the FDR Drive. Just off of Wards Island, Dawes and I moved side by side, picking up speed. After a while, I glanced back, wanting to keep an eye on Sue. "She's in the river," I said, and we swooped around.

While Dawes went through the steps of a T-rescue, Sue treaded water and explained she had dropped her water bottle. When she reached to pick it up, she rolled into the water.

Dawes pulled Sue's boat perpendicular to his own and rolled it over to drain out the water. He then righted the boat and placed it parallel to his. He stabilized Sue's kayak so she could get back in. Sue inserted her feet into the cockpit and executed a sit-up right into the boat. Her move would have won a gold medal.

When we pulled out to rest on Randall Island, which has been connected by fill with Wards Island, Sue, her black shoulder-length hair plastered to her head, was shivering. The water had warmed to about 67 degrees, but chill comes quickly below 70.

Soon, a police officer arrived. "We got a call saying some kid fell into the river. Everything OK?"

We thanked him. That we were being looked out for delighted me.

I ate an orange and my second peanut-butter sandwich while we watched two teams play soccer. Too soon, we packed up. The sun was heading west, and we knew we were going to finish our paddle in the dark, so we attached our lights to the back of our boats.

Sue announced she never wanted to get in a kayak again, so we were not stopping at the railroad bridge at Spuyten Duyvil. That meant I had to pee there on Randall's Island. As I hid behind a bush, I remembered how when I walked in the city finding public restrooms was a problem. I never would have squatted, even in the parks, but somehow my kayak and this whole endeavor allowed me any behavior.

"I found a present for you," Dawes greeted me on my return. On top of my kayak sat a DVD case: *Big Butt, Road Trip 4. Monster butt certified. Shot on location.* I wondered what location.

"This is great," I said. Porn—not wildlife—was more what I had expected to find circling the city.

High on the East River, I saw people walking on paths next to the river. One woman leaned over the railing, and waved. "Paddle safely," she called. We turned into the eight-mile-long Harlem River, a strait that separates Manhattan and the Bronx. The waters were calm—we had the currents just right—as we paddled toward two men fishing. Just as we approached we saw one man's pole bend with a catch. We slowed to watch him reel in a white undershirt.

We scooted past a wall of Inwood marble. The white marble was smeared black by time and pollution. The narrow strait was tinged with a bit of melancholy as the last licks of light filtered through to us at Baker Field, where Columbia University athletes train and compete. They also have a crew team, and I could see how in these smooth waters a racing shell would move beautifully. A large Jordy blue *C* is painted on a rock beneath the railroad tracks.

Darkness had settled in for good by the time we reached Spuyten Duyvil, another name that invokes fear. One translation is "devil's whirlpool," though the creek that caused the whirlpools has been filled.

We twisted on our bright white lights and dug under the final bridge, a railroad swing bridge. Before us spread a mile expanse of the Hudson River, calm as the ebb tide was beginning its pull. There was not a boat visible in either direction. We spotted the light at the Englewood Marina and pushed onto the dark, smooth river toward our original launch. South of us the George Washington Bridge lit the sky, and Manhattan glowed orange-yellow. None of the city noise reached us on our watery way, and so the city took on a luminous, holy appearance. An odd, elated sense of peace wrapped us there in the middle of the river; overwhelmed by the miracle of it all, our fatigue floated off.

We coasted onto the darkened beach. For a while I sat in my boat, unable to exit or pack up as Dawes ran for the car and Sue dismantled her paddles. I didn't want to let go of what lay behind me: 10,000 strokes, eight and a half hours, twenty-eight miles, two peanut-butter sandwiches. I knew then that it was still possible to have one perfect day.

16

NUBIAN GOATS

I talked a lot about my dead man, referring to him as *my* dead man. I mentioned him to colleagues; I described him at dinner parties and to anyone who asked, innocently, "How are you?" Where the conversation led astonished me. Everyone has a plan about the best way to die.

My mother did not choose her death, but, still, I had started to think of her death as right. She was sick for not too long, but long enough that friends and family traveled from far away to say good-bye. I hold onto this to counter regrets, which I feared would overwhelm me. Why had we subjected her to the radiation and chemotherapy, why had we made her final months a medical marathon? And, we were never able to deliver on her last requests to see her friends Mardee and Phil, or her wish to return to France one last time. I did not want to dwell on what we had not been able to do. My father had been at her side for hours every day telling her that he loved her. He, Becky, and I had been there to tell her we were glad she was there.

In July we carried half of my mother's ashes in a ceramic urn to Estampes. We gathered the villagers, her French friends, and relatives over a lunch, and then said a Mass in the small church. It was a beautiful day, and the church bells rang through the valley. In the distance we could see the Pyrenees, the summits of the highest peaks still cloaked in snow. We walked to the graveyard down the hill to the family tomb. Our neighbor Odette was at my side. I had spent many summers working in the fields alongside Odette, baling hay and taking the cows to pasture. Those summers that I was in the house alone, she fed me. I think of her as a second mother. I reached for her hand, strong and rough from a life of farming. I held tight, needing her strength.

The local undertaker, big-bellied, cheerful Gascon, had opened the family tomb the day before. He pushed aside the tibia of my great-grandparents, Montegut, lying bare there inside the bulky stone grave.

"There's a box here," he said.

"What box?" my father asked.

"It looks like a box of cookies," he said in a cheerful voice.

We smiled at each other, puzzled. "Oh, that is our grandmother," I said. My grandmother in a cookie box there with her parents. We had giggled about it all evening, imitating the undertaker's voice, "Une boîte de gâteaux—A box of cookies." How different he was from the gloomy undertakers in State College.

After the service, we stood together, kissed the urn filled with Jacquie's ashes, and placed it in the tomb. Knowing my mother was where she belonged made me calmer. Almost one year after her death, the grief had dissipated, just as everyone said it would. If I had been living with a loss of eleven on a scale of one to twelve, I had now moved to a seven.

◊ ◊ ◊

My dead man did not make me hesitant about the river. Rather, I wanted to venture out even more. Perhaps I could wash away the image of his body, prone on shore. At the same time, I developed a new fear. Like the climber who did not want to fall, I became the kayaker who does not want to drown. I decided that what I needed was to take a class to learn to roll.

I'd read a book on rolling; I watched a video. How to make this happen did not make sense in the absence of practice, so on a Saturday I drove down to the kayak center in Annsville, where I had taken a class two years earlier. The instructor went over the basics, and then we were in the water. He stood to my side as I lay my body against my boat, lined my paddle up to the side, and toppled over.

Each time, I sputtered to the surface, desperate for air.

"How do you feel about your hang time?" the instructor finally asked.

My hang time? Hang time is the amount of time a person can hang upside down in their boat before the need for air takes over.

"I feel awful about my hang time," I joked. Really, it is not natural to hang upside down in a boat in the water. Shouldn't I want to clamber toward air? Instead, he wanted me to hang as long as possible until I tapped my boat and he righted me.

I finally understood that the essential strength came from my hips, a definite snap that brought my torso to the surface. The sweep of the paddle across the surface of the water was secondary. But before I figured this out, I had water shoot up my nose and had wrenched my neck as I tried to bring my head up too soon. It was too much to ask that after hanging upside down my head was supposed to be the last thing out of the water. I left the course with a decent hang time and the clear knowledge that rolling was not a skill I could count on.

◊ ◊ ◊

On a weekend, I traveled north about an hour, deciding to put in near Castleton, on the eastern shore. I pulled down the long drive into Schodack Island State Park (pronounced Sko-dack), passing under both the Castleton Bridge, which connects the Berkshires with the New York State Thruway, and the steel structure of the Alfred H. Smith Memorial Bridge, a railroad bridge. Since 1974, when the Poughkeepsie railroad bridge burned, the Alfred H. Smith Memorial Bridge has been the southernmost crossing for freight trains.

Schodack Island is in fact a peninsula, with 1,052 acres of forested land and seven miles of shoreline. The park offers more amenities than any landing I had visited on the river: bathrooms, a soda machine, hiking trails, a boat launch, and interpretive signs. A dozen cars with trailers stood in the parking lot.

I pointed my kayak south, following the edge of Schodack Island. Schodack means "place of fire," as it is said the Mohicans kept a permanent fire on the island. The island connects with Houghtaling Island to the south. These islands buffered me from the railroads. But this did not mean that I had silence. Boys on dirt bikes raced back and forth along the sandy shoreline, the rev and roar of their engines echoing in the trees.

Just across the river was the Blue Circle Cement plant, which, from a distance, looked like an old rickety barn perched atop an ultramodern steel base. A spindly contraption soared into the air to load limestone onto barges. But the way it disappeared into the sky I thought it might off-load clouds.

Further south on the western shore more industry bellied up to the river. What looked like a section of a steel bridge stood on a barge. I learned later that this was the new Willis Avenue Bridge that would parade by barge down the river to its new home connecting Manhattan and the Bronx. Signs near the water read Avoid Finger Amputation. This industry on the western shore in Albany County stared across at the pristine shores of Schodack Island in Rensselaer County.

In this narrow stretch of river—little over a thousand yards wide—pleasure boats whipped by, often towing a water-skier. These small boats created wakes that tossed me about. The river had a summertime feel to it. I saw boaters, kids on their dirt bikes, rope swings suspended from trees near shore, fishermen, and a couple sunbathing. I was so struck by this—never had I seen anyone sunbathe on the banks of the Hudson—that I paddled nearer to be sure I was correct. At first I thought I saw two very large dogs with the couple, seated in their folding chairs. But soon the animals took shape: long legs, floppy ears, deer-sized. I paddled closer to be sure my eyes were not deceiving me.

"Are those your goats?" I asked. My voice carried across the small span of water.

He pulled down his glasses and looked up from his book. "Yes," he said.

"Are they Nubian goats?"

"Yes," he said again.

I paddled on, smiling.

On my return I pulled over on the western shore, just north of Coeymans (pronounced Kwee-mens). Throughout the valley, bricks litter the shoreline. Most are broken. Some are intact, the frog mark—the name of the company raised in the center of the brick—distinct. At this landing, I turned over bricks with the frog marks SSBCO and P&M. Powell and Minnock was the last brickyard to close on the Hudson. When it shut its doors in 2001, a trade that began in 1630 came to an end. SSBCO is Sutton and Suderly, the largest yard at Coeymans. Both companies were part of the heyday of the brick industry, which peaked at the turn of the twentieth century with 130 brickyards in operation. Brick making extended the length of the river, with the greatest number of brickyards in Ulster County—in a sixteen-mile stretch above the city of Kingston, there were twenty yards. In this section of the river near Coeymans, there were ten brickyards.

The kilns where they dried the bricks—made from the clay soil, mixed with sand and coal dust—were housed under enormous wooden sheds. These large sheds were built alongside the river so that the bricks could be loaded onto barges and shipped downriver. Crumbling brick-making buildings have long been part of the landscape. In 1939, Carmer wrote that both sides of the Hudson were lined with "the picturesque weathered ruins of many yards, their chimneys standing lonely beside tumbled, weed-grown walls and staring, empty windows." But in his day the brick-laden barges were still making their way down the river from fifty active brickyards. "At night the river beside the dark, low-lying silhouettes of the yards glows dully with the eerie light of the brickyard fires." Nathaniel Parker Willis, writing in the mid-nineteenth century, was less enthusiastic: "Brickyards are our eyesore in the scenery of the Highlands."

Silhouettes in eerie light, or eyesore? I found it sad that this industry had died, for a range of reasons: depleted clay deposits, poor management, expensive production costs, and less demand. I paddled past the Powell and Minnock kiln sheds, which are made of steel. A long, drooping crane juts out over the water. Not long after my paddle, an enterprising man bought the Powell and Minnock sheds with dreams of using them to start up new industry. I hope it thrives, because though I love my green stretches of river, I also know that industry and nature rubbing shoulders is the essential energy of this valley.

As I paddled back to the dock I saw something that I had lived my whole life waiting to see: an osprey plummeting from the sky to catch a fish. It was dazzling to watch the speed at which it dove, feet first, toward the water. The osprey then took flight, a fish grasped like a bayonet in its talons.

Back home, I called my father, as I now did almost every day. I told him first about the osprey. Then, "I saw a couple sunbathing with pet Nubian goats."

He laughed. "Susie, you are making that up."

"No, I saw it."

"Dead men, now this."

I heard something in my father's voice and in my own: we were both coming back to life.

"That's the Hudson River," I said.

17

STURGEON MOON

Mark Twain said you could not see enough sunrises on the Mississippi. I think you cannot see enough sunsets on the Hudson. On my
reach off Tivoli, at the end of a hot August day the sun plunged behind the Catskills, orange and yellow, casting shadows from behind
clouds that stuttered across the sky. It was hard not to feel a bit desperate watching the sun go down. *Slow down,* I wanted to say. *Wait, just
a second. Let's back up and do that again.* But off it went, dropping out of
sight, then casting a magical, even embarrassing, afterglow that illuminated the east. Matching this was the moon, rising majestically above
the eastern shore.

I looped south, idling on the west side of Magdalen Island where
the water runs deep, to forty-seven feet, and the barges snug in close.
In that miraculous afterglow—a pink tinged everything in the west
while to the south pastel blues and purples swirled in the sky, like
a perfect watercolor—I saw in the distance seven enormous white
dots. I slushed across a field of submerged vegetation, a mix of celery
and spatterdock, rich and thick at that point in the season. A narrow

open passage allowed me to get closer to the glowing beacons. And as I approached they took on the shape of mute swans, necks curved graciously.

Mute swans are not native to this region and they are not mute, making a rough-edged honking noise. These swans were descended from domestic swans brought to grace the ponds of river estates. Those had escaped, bred, and thrived, thanks in part to people who feed them. They are beautiful, large birds, with elegant curved necks. Who wouldn't want to toss them some stale bread? And that is what people do, off of the docks of small towns up and down the river. Yet many are also unhappy with these birds—their beauty doesn't cancel out that they are invasive, like the zebra mussel or water chestnut— and their aggressive behavior challenges other waterfowl. There on the river in the near dark they looked mystical. Then I paddled too close, frightening them. As they took off, the sound of their wings brushing the water made a powerful whoosh.

Sunset leads inevitably to night. I was drawn to the darkness of the river, wanted to know my reach by feel, by scent. I had the idea that to fully experience the night, I couldn't launch in daylight, I had to begin and end my paddle in darkness. I waited a few days before undertaking this outing; I waited for the August full moon, the Sturgeon Moon. Native Americans named the full moons to keep track of the seasons. Fishing tribes are credited with naming the Sturgeon Moon: August was the month to easily catch a sturgeon. I didn't want to catch a sturgeon; I wanted to paddle, imagining their long, sleek bodies curving just below my boat.

At eleven o'clock, I slid my boat off of my car and into the water. The landing at the end of Tivoli was deserted and dark, despite the moon, which was enormous, a glowing ivory ball with the mottling of its surface visible. I could see canyons and mountains, a vivid lunar topography.

I stroked out onto the water, which reflected the moonlight like a silver platter. Very quickly a vertiginous feeling took over. In the dark, the shallows became a watery abyss, the bed of the river now hundreds of feet beneath me. The surface of the water, shiny smooth in calm wind, had pockets where it swirled and shifted to the movements of creatures from below that ached to leap out and snatch me, taking me under to my sturgeon life. These were childhood fears—the monster under the bed ready to grab my feet—in a grown-up cloak. But I knew they were not innocent. If I let these thoughts take over, they would chase me back onto land. I pushed through my night fear, and when I emerged I was weaving south toward Magdalen Island. With each stroke I tried to get a sense of my movement. Despite my efforts, my paddle dipping methodically into the river, the lights on shore did not shift. I stroked some more until, gradually, the yellow streetlights of Tivoli faded.

A cloudless sky made for an even, spectacular light, with impenetrable shadows near shore. When I approached the shoreline, I was surrounded by an immense pool of India ink below, and a cool delicate black blanket above. So I ventured further out in the river to be in the light of the moon. There, the light settled on my shoulders, shimmered on the hull of my boat.

I heard a splash as a fish returned to the river after vaulting into the air. My face and arms felt the pinprick of bugs striking me. I kept my mouth shut, not wanting to swallow any of those bugs. The air felt warm and smooth, and from time to time I passed through a cooler pocket of air that washed my face. I scooched toward the riverside of Magdalen. The island was a quiet, dark presence. Katydids sang their song out of the dark forest. In the distance were the regular yellow lights that dot the span of the Kingston Bridge. On the western shore, a few lights told me that some in Glasco were still awake.

As I ebbed around the end of Magdalen Island a large bird dropped out of a tree and sailed toward North Tivoli Bay, making a loud croaking noise that shattered the night. I stopped paddling for a moment to watch the heron's heavy wing beats.

In the hundred-yard stretch of river between land and the island, I knew where to move to avoid the spatterdock on the one side and the grasses on the other. Making my way through the maze of water plants, I emerged to the sight of a fiery series of lights and the low rumble of a tug, towing a long barge, its silhouette barely visible. The parade of red, yellow, and white lights reflected as ribbons on the water. I felt the tug whoosh past, leaving behind a deep wake. I rode the waves, the bow of my boat gently rising and falling.

Paddling under the Sturgeon Moon was disorienting and a bit hallucinatory. My thoughts didn't just wander; they leapt. I went from memories of my mother (soft sadness) to anticipating the first day of classes fast approaching (mild anxiety) to reflecting on my recent time in France (bittersweet pleasure) to focusing on the lights of Glasco on the far shore (what were people doing there?). My mind settled on contemplating what those sturgeon were doing deep under the water, their enormous bodies snaking along, full of their power. What would it be to join them on their cold, secret journeys back in time? This tack of thought was as dizzying as the swirls of water around me.

I wanted to become one with the night, to enter my sturgeon life, one where I would be strong and unshakable, as sure of my design as a sturgeon is of hers. But I knew this would take time. I would need to go out night after night until the movement of water and light began to make sense, until I experienced what I do during the day: that the river cradles me. This also took time. When I first slipped into my kayak in the daytime I felt the hard fiberglass division between me and what moved beneath me. Now I feel as if I'm in the water, as if it, not the wrap of the boat, holds me. At night my sense of the river was different. With the moon beaming down on me, patches of cool air intermixed with warm currents caressing my face, creating the illusion of a magnificent ice rink. My movement in my kayak was often tentative. When I leaned into a turn, I became unbalanced so fast, and shifted to center again in a snap. The river that night tolerated me.

When I pulled into the landing at Tivoli, I prided myself on knowing just where rocks emerged so I could land without scraping the bottom of my boat. The landing was empty, the lights from Friendship Street offering a yellow glow to the white of the moon.

At one in the morning I slid into my sheets. On the wall of my bedroom hangs a photo of the fisherman Tucker Crawford with a 200-pound sturgeon draped across his rowboat. He looks casual, a cigarette dangling from his mouth. The fish lies limp after great battle, dwarfing the boat. I understood how brave that fish had been. I had been out there but a few hours, facing the dizzying dark and all that it holds. It had been out there for hundreds of nights, working its way through the purple-black, dark as thought. I slept hard and well, preparing for a new life.

18

SITTING BY THE RIVER

There are some things I do not like to do alone: watch movies, either in a theater or at home; attend a concert; eat a delicious dinner; sit by the river. But there I was on March 23, 2007, alone on a half-damp log on the banks of the Hudson River at the Tivoli landing. There was not a cloud over the river, leaving a dome of blue. Yet over the Catskills, clouds bunched, and the mountains settled in like a herd of sleeping camels. Quite simply it was beautiful.

It had been a while since I had been on the river. I had stopped paddling in October when I discovered a bone spur in my neck that left me with constant headaches. Heaving a boat around did not help, so I had, by the late fall, given up my river outings. Something happened to me without the river. For one thing, I had lots of time. Lots. I cleaned my basement, threw away clothes that should have been tossed years ago. My silver spoons shone after a good polish. I stripped the baseboard radiator of dust. In other words, I was bored out of my mind.

And in this boredom something awful happened. I stopped seeing the world. I no longer noticed the wind or the color of the sky as vividly as I did when I imagined I could be on the water. On the water, I am alert—to wind, to the shift in temperatures that mean rain, to the color of the world. And in this alert state I see Canada geese migrating, monarch butterflies on their extraordinary path south, and flowers trying to push forth their final colors. I realized that paddling had trained me to see the world, because on the water seeing matters.

When I try to explain to people that my paddling is about living, this is what I mean: going out onto the river is about staying alert to the richness of the world; it's about striving to live.

◊ ◊ ◊

My father visited one late October weekend, to distract me from my pain. We drove up to Olana, Frederic Church's house high above the river. When we stepped out of the car my father looked at the house with its turrets and inlaid roof. Rather than say "Wow" in amazement, he said, "Dear Lord," appalled by the ornate architecture. The red brick home was inspired by a trip Church took to Persia, and the interior reflects those same influences, with open rooms that allow light to stream in. The windows frame the landscape, which spreads to the south. To the west is a view Church never would have seen: the Rip Van Winkle Bridge, opened in 1935, which takes people to Catskill.

Still, from Church's vantage, I saw much of what he had seen, the vastness of the sky and of the river. The sunsets over the Catskills were, I now knew, often as rich as he had painted them. Church's paintings were faithful to the landscape—or, as faithful as one can be when duplicating the natural world.

My father and I drove across the Rip Van Winkle Bridge and continued inland toward Woodstock to wander amidst Harvey Fite's fantastic Opus 40. Created out of bluestone, one stone piled artfully on top of the next, Opus 40 is a series of moats and platforms that swirl together, inviting people to explore, and get lost in intimate passageways. We were pulled toward the centerpiece, the eight-ton, foursquare chunk of rock that rises fifteen feet high. How one man—both visionary and obsessive—did all of this is hard to grasp, even knowing he spent thirty-seven years at it. During that time he was also teaching sculpture at Bard College. Fite died crushed by his mower when it went over the edge of his sculpture and landed in one of the moats.

On another day, my father and I visited several monasteries on the western shore of the river. We explored Mount St. Alphonsus, the blocky monastery that hangs over the river across from Norrie Point. Built in 1900, it once housed an order of Roman Catholic Redemptorists. We found the doors open, and so walked light-footed down the high-ceilinged hallways. We whispered to each other, wondering if we were allowed to peer behind wooden doors to look into the sparsely furnished rooms. Once back out in the fresh air we wondered aloud who lived there and why it was so empty.

We drove down narrow, twisting roads south of Port Ewen to visit John Burroughs's home, named Slabsides. Burroughs is the valley's most famous naturalist writer. When I first discovered Burroughs he disappointed me. I had hoped for a keen early twentieth-century vision of this region, to find a real voice for this river. But in all of his many essays only one, "A River View," is about the Hudson. In it he writes: "The Hudson is a long arm of the sea, and it has something of the sea's austerity and grandeur. I think one might spend a lifetime upon its banks without feeling any sense of ownership in it, or becoming at all intimate with it: it keeps one at arm's length."

I worried that if Burroughs could not find intimacy with the river, my chances were slim. But the key words in Burroughs are "lifetime upon its banks." If he had just built himself a raft and set afloat on the river, perhaps he would have found the intimacy he was looking for.

Burroughs is very little read these days, though he wrote over thirty books and in his lifetime (born in 1837; died in 1921) was popular. He was friends or was acquainted with many of the literary and political men of his time: poet Walt Whitman, naturalist John Muir, and President Teddy Roosevelt. Henry Ford gave him a Model T, in part to keep him quiet about cars, afraid he would condemn them as "steel monsters." He grew up in the same town and was friends with Jay Gould, the railroad magnate. These disparate yet connected lives show two paths of the time: toward innovation and progress or back to the natural world. These contrasting impulses are not dissimilar to the choices people are making today. Still, Burroughs's words do not resonate.

His long, complicated sentences, similar to those of Emerson (some of Burroughs's early work was thought to be plagiarized from Emerson), took me a while to settle into. Coupled with this complex sentence structure is prose that verges (like that of his friend John Muir) on the ecstatic. So often we get "remarkable days," "a day of great beauty," "days of great freshness and beauty," "perfect day," "brilliant day." Since I too love those brilliant days, I eventually gave over to Burroughs's writing, and forgave him that he focused on the Catskill Mountains, not the Hudson River, as subject. Mountains or river, his eye was trained on the natural world in wonderful ways; nothing can rival his descriptions of birdcalls. But what I love most in his work is that his emotions—he is often admittedly moody—play out in relation to what he sees and hears in the natural world. "The finest fox sparrow song I ever heard. How it went to my sad heart!" he writes on April 10, 1881, in his journals. And throughout his work it is clear that he holds to his own advice: "Unless you can write about Nature with feeling, with real love, with more or less hearty affiliation and comradeship with her, it is no use. Your words will not stick." He loves the natural world.

Church with his Persian manor, Fite and his endless rocks, Burroughs deep in the woods with his birds—the region is uncommonly rich in eccentrics.

As my father had done my whole life, during his visit he reawakened me to the beauty of the world, the quirkiness of people, and the fun of discovery.

◊ ◊ ◊

Forty feet out, ice chunks moved north, while flotillas of ice clustered near shore, swirling with the grace of elephants. The floes took on shapes so that as I sat on shore I imagined a range of creatures. An otter on a floe. A fox. A beaver riding a chunk of ice.

The current was shifting. The water near shore changes direction first, followed by the deeper water midriver. I know this from paddling, how those currents near shore have unexpectedly pushed me the wrong direction. But knowing something is different from seeing something. I know there are currents, but I don't see them unless a stick is tossed in the water or ice dances north or south. It's like knowing the wind and seeing the wind, how it shuffles tree branches and raises dust. It's like knowing love and seeing love tucked into a delicious meal.

I was half-carefree, my bottom damp and a bit cold. What had revived me after the fall was a January cross-country trip to Arizona with my father. We stopped in Danville, Kentucky, to visit my grandparents' graves, to look at "grandmother's house" on Mildred Court, and admire the Fox home with its long columns. We drove past the farm where my father had spent many of his summers, and the changes to the property made him wish we had not. I heard my father's voice become animated as we entered the Blue Ridge Mountains, which were full of family stories, like that of George Rogers Clark, who fought in the Revolutionary War. He loved his roots in Kentucky, the Foxes who owned land and the Gists who were lawyers. Through these stories, I understood that all of this was our land, though we did not live there any longer.

We made a looping trip, south from Kentucky into Tennessee, through Mississippi and Louisiana, before slowing our pace a bit in Texas to explore the Gulf Coast. We veered off the highway to visit places with names like Pinch, Enterprise, and Alice just because we could and it pleased us. We both had a keen awareness that Jacquie was not with us. When we sent off a postcard, ate a good meal, spoken and unspoken was our sadness that she was not there to share with us. And then together we laughed, realizing that if she were alive, she would not have joined us on this trip. The car made her sleepy, and when not sleeping, she focused on the crossword puzzle while my father would point out with some frustration, "Look at this, that." Her curiosity was not for rows of FEMA trailers outside of New Orleans or billboards about God, but for people. My father was aware of his new freedom. It was not what he would have chosen, but it offered some ballast to the loneliness he had sunk into. Life goes on, she so often said. With hesitation and sadness, we both saw that she was right.

The movement across country was a tonic for us both. In every town my father sniffed out the used bookstores while I went on long walks. We spent Christmas with old friends near Chattanooga—Jeanine Peterson, who with her husband, Don, had introduced my parents in 1956 in Iowa City. We stopped to eat oysters in New Orleans and then tried to spy whooping cranes at the Aransas National Wildlife Refuge in Texas. We crossed many rivers, including the Ohio and Mississippi. We looked down on the Tennessee River from atop Signal Mountain outside of Chattanooga. We also wandered beside the Rio Grande in Texas. They are all lovely rivers, but it became clear, as we admired these great flows, that the Hudson was the only river for me. Like a woman who has found her love, I could admire these rivers, but my heart was taken.

In Arizona we set up shop in a rented condo at the base of Sabino Canyon. From there, we continued to comb used bookstores, but we also walked into Sabino Canyon to picnic, watched Preston Sturges films in the evening, and enjoyed my father's new skills in the kitchen. He had learned to whip up a great stir-fry, and one day I returned from a daylong hike to find short ribs in the oven.

My father then drove home from Arizona alone while I flew back. Every day he called in with progress on his trip: a stop at the Lonesome Dove bookstore in Archer City, Texas, where he acquired a few more boxes of books; a stop in St. Louis to see his cousin Anne, whom he found required an oxygen tank in order to breathe. He drove through snow and storms, and I could tell he felt heroic by the end of the trip.

◊ ◊ ◊

Sitting on the bank of my river, I was looking forward to the summer, to a different heat than the heat of the desert. I wanted to organize the summer around the Hudson, exploring the upper reaches or the tributaries, especially the Rondout, which runs out by Kingston. Back in August, I had paddled a ways into the Rondout to mark the anniversary of my mother's death. The range of boats in the hidden marinas intrigued me. I wanted to loiter in Ramshorn Marsh just south of Catskill and learn the birds there. Maybe I would paddle the length of the river in one push. Once again I felt I could do anything.

How fast things change.

My father would die in nine days. I did not know this, of course, as I sat there so content in the sun by the river. I was innocent, imagining that I had all the time in the world to plan my little outings, and that was all that mattered. The river feeds that illusion, moving back and forth in its regular extended heartbeat. Rivers serve many purposes, and this is one, to give the sense of eternity in its regular patterns. After all, the Tigris and Euphrates that issue from the Garden of Eden still flow. I imagined my father would live as long as the river ebbed and flowed.

On Sunday morning, still in my pajamas, I was collecting my *New York Times* delivered to my house, bundled in its blue plastic sleeve, when a sheriff pulled in front of my house. He backed up and tucked into the driveway. My first thought was, *What did I do wrong?*

"Is this the Rogers residence?" he asked.

I nodded, my breath catching.

"I have bad news about your father in central Pennsylvania."

At those words, my legs gave out beneath me. The sheriff crouched and gathered me up, half-carrying me into the house.

He sat with me for a while, then asked, "Isn't there someone I can call to come sit with you?" The person I wanted was my sister, living far away in France.

"I'm OK," I said. He sat with me a while longer, witness to my tears, and then left, a kind man burdened with bringing bad news.

I did not quite believe what the sheriff had told me. I called the hospital in State College. "Are you sure it's Thomas Rogers?" I asked. And I still didn't believe it. It was April 1, April Fool's Day. Was it possible this was a cruel joke?

I dialed Becky's phone number. Her daughter Alice answered the phone, cheerful at hearing my voice. "I need your mother, Alice," I said.

"She's in the bath," Alice said. "Can she call you back?"

"No." I couldn't help myself. "Dadi is dead," I said, using the name she used for her beloved grandfather.

Becky was already crying when she got to the phone. Together we wailed our loss, the phone lines echoing across an ocean. That night, my cousin Lisa drove up from New Jersey with baskets of food to hug me and share my tears. Then the next day I drove to State College. Becky had gotten on the first flight out of Paris and arrived a short hour after I did. We wrapped our arms around each other in the lobby of the small airport and wept openly. The house smelled of dust as we wandered room to room, absorbing the emptiness. We opened the refrigerator and found it stocked with food left by neighbors. The doorbell rang, and our neighbor Ron stood there with lasagna. He told us that he had gathered with a few friends and neighbors the night before to drink martinis and tell stories of Tom. While they sat drinking, a reporter from the *Centre Daily Times* had called, wanting information, some words to add to the article they ran the next day on the front page. "We passed the phone around," Ron said, "and at the end the reporter said, 'Well, have a nice day.'" We all laughed.

The next morning, Becky and I drove to the funeral home to see our father's body, long and unmoving. We touched his cold hard cheek. There is knowing death, and there is seeing death.

◊ ◊ ◊

What happened to the river in the nine days between when I sat there watching it flow by and the day my father died? The ice cleared out. The water flowed by. It accepted some garbage to carry into the bays; it left some garbage on shore.

What did I do? I taught classes. I ate breakfast. I walked to the river. I also put my boat in the water for the first time for the season. There was excitement and trepidation as I, slick in a wet suit, returned to water so cold it took my breath away. Paddling north then south, my body eased into the regular motion, accepted the ache in my lower back as I refamiliarized myself with the motions of kayaking. The freedom I find on the river spread before me. All of this I recall in broad, impressionistic swaths. But in the other minutes of other hours of those nine days, little stands out in detail.

Yet I do remember one moment vividly. I called my father near ten at night on March 31. There was no reason for the call except I wanted to hear his voice. He sounded low, sitting there in his study at his large leather-topped desk playing solitaire. After our cross-country trip he had fallen into a slump made deeper by news of his cousin Anne's death. He was tired from too many hours of gardening, the tulips already in bloom. But I knew what was going on. He was lonely. Soon, though, we were both laughing, as we so often did.

"You've cheered me up," he said.

I will forever hear his voice flecked with a bit of lightness, the texture of his laugh. I cheered him up on the night before he died.

And then the next morning he woke, knew that his heart was not ticking properly. He packed his toilet kit with his medications and slipped on his gray blue parka we had bought together. Was he frightened as he drove toward the hospital? This is what haunts me: The image of my father grasping the steering wheel of his little Mazda with both hands, a bit hunched over, urging the car forward, hoping to get to safety on time. His heart beat erratically, hesitated until it gave one final push, flailed, expired. His car veered off the road. He was two minutes from the hospital. At 7:15 he was dead.

I have much to learn about death, but what I know is this: mother and father are both gone, and alone takes on new meaning. What I had felt as alone in the past was but a shadow. This alone was not just an emotion; it defied gravity. I anchored myself in this world through my parents. Without them, it all felt so small, so fragile. Without them, I would sit through movies, concerts, and good meals alone. I would sit by the river alone.

19

GOLDEN CLUB

In the weeks after my father's death venturing onto the river by myself left me uneasy. When I did, I thought too much about how long it would be before someone sent out alerts if I were to slip into the river. But this, really, was a way to feel sorry for myself, to indulge my sense of isolation. Still, my emotional caution kept me more landbound. So on a hot day in late May I decided on a walk to Cruger Island to search out golden club.

Cruger Island is a paramecium-shaped piece of land just off of the Bard College campus, separating North and South Tivoli Bays. A causeway connects the island to the mainland. Portions of the causeway are submerged at high tide, but at low tide it is possible to walk out to the island, though it is best to wear rubber boots. On the northeast side of the island in marshy land grows a rare plant called golden club. I am not someone who knows every plant in the woods— far from it. What intrigued me about golden club is that it is rare. To see this rare plant, I needed to go look for it in the two weeks that it blooms.

I drove to the campus, passing the small gatehouse that serves as the offices of the college's international programs. I had just read about the gatehouse in Carmer's *The Hudson*. During the 1850s a man named Orson Squire Fowler became famous for his ideas on phrenology. He would read clients' skulls, telling if they were "endowed with generous, niggardly or proper amounts of Ideality, Eventuality, Amativeness, or Philoprogenitiveness." After making a fortune telling people if they would be licentious or frigid (one's amativeness) or produce a lot of offspring (one's philoprogenitiveness), he turned to architecture (of course!), proclaiming the wonders of an eight-sided house. An eight-sided house comes close to being a sphere, which is beautiful and encloses the most space with the least material. And, there is more sunlight. Many octagonal houses still stand in the valley as a reminder of Fowler and the power of his ideas. Carmer claims the gatehouse is an offspring of Fowler's ideas. I pulled over to admire and walk around the building only to discover it has six sides, not eight.

I parked near Blithewood Manor. It is not an old mansion, but rather one built in 1900. Still, it has that Old World feeling. Students circulate stories of the ghosts that haunt its hallways. Blithewood now houses the Levy Economics Institute—perhaps to scare off those ghosts—and on the rolling lawns around it students play Ultimate Frisbee, strum guitars, and nap in the spring sunshine. Just two weeks earlier the graduation tent stood at this spot, celebrating and ushering out yet another class of students. The semester was over, and though my grades were still due, I was relieved that before me stretched a few months in which I could reorient myself in the world. I had the sense that with my father's death things should stop, or at least slow down. But the pace of life continued. Some of it felt overwhelming; some of it I welcomed. Just three weeks earlier, I had danced at Emmet's wedding. At first, I was puzzled why he was getting married so young, and then as I watched him kiss his bride on May 17 I saw how the sailor boy no longer needed to wander. I could see a baby on the near horizon. I admired that he was able to throw his whole heart into his life. Before him rested years in which to sink roots into the rich Massachusetts soil where he and his young wife had decided to settle on a Christmas tree farm.

Below Blithewood is one of my favorite spots on the Bard campus, the formal Italian-style garden, lush with wisteria in the spring and with lavender in the summer. A small fountain adds a calming cascade to this contained setting. The view from the end of the garden looks over the expanse of South Tivoli Bay. Unlike North Bay, with its intimate cattail-lined water paths, South Bay is an open expanse of water. In winter it freezes over, and iceboats glide on the smooth surface. At low tide, it becomes a mud flat. In this exposed bay is a tiny rock island, Skillpot, where a few tenacious columbine pop into bloom every spring. By midsummer the bay is so thick with water chestnut that paddling is impossible. For this reason, I have ventured into South Bay but a half dozen times in the early spring.

I dove into the woods, carrying a knapsack filled with bread, cheese, and water. The narrow mud path, heavy with clay, roamed over the hills in the woods, which are dense with oaks, sugar maple, beech, and, from time to time, a stand of hemlock. A walk in the woods—what could be more normal? That was what I was desperate for. In such moments I could see beyond my desolation to the wide-leafed shiny skunk cabbage, the rectangular hole made by a pileated woodpecker, and the yellow trout lilies. Too quickly, though, everything looped back to my father. He was a spring gardener, glorying in flowers that grew wild beside the path, like trillium, hepatica, and jack-in-the-pulpit. He had several jack-in-the-pulpit in a shaded section in his garden. I pictured him folding his long frame to plant level, brushing away a few overlapping leaves and then lifting the hood of the plant to reveal jack there in his pulpit.

Did he know of golden club? Probably not. But I was sure if he did he would have wanted to come with me on this venture. I had just discovered the existence of golden club three days earlier. I read about it in Esther Kiviat's book on Tivoli Bays. The draw to see golden club was not about its beauty—the photo made it look like a yellow riding crop sticking up from broad velvety leaves. Why I wanted to see it was more complicated.

To walk just to walk is one thing, a pleasure. But to walk with a destination transforms the walk into a quest. This too I got from my father via that great mystery called genes. But it wasn't just the natural world that guided my father's outings. When he carted our family through France, he often strayed far off the beaten track to see rare statues or stained-glass windows in intimate Romanesque churches. Standing before a particularly beautiful sight—a statue or a view of the mountains—he would beam or at times cry, his responses strong and pure. I had a keen desire to recreate that sense of discovery.

I stopped at a promontory that has been given the name of Buttock's Island (even though it is not an island), and looked out at a dozen great blue heron, scattered through the bay, wading in the shallow water or standing in utter stillness, waiting to spear a fish. After twenty minutes of walking north, I emerged at a carriage road that led due west out to the island. This was where horse carriages plodded, taking John Church Cruger to his island when he purchased it in 1835.

Cruger adds his own colorful story to the valley. Fascinated by ruins and the past, he built stone arches on South Cruger Island and placed Mayan figures inside of them. These limestone works were a gift of the American explorer John Lloyd Stephens. The foundation of the arches is all that is left on South Cruger, but earlier travelers on the river were greeted by these exotic figures from the Yucatán.

When Cruger bought the island, it was named Magdalen. He imposed his name on the island and bumped the name of Magdalen north, onto Goat Island. Naming an island is one sure way of making a place your own. Since Rogers is such a common name, there are already two Rogers Islands in the river. One is off Fort Edward, near where General Electric dumped PCBs into the river. It is a big island and was a major British encampment during the French and Indian War. The other lies just south of the city of Hudson under the Rip Van Winkle Bridge. I've paddled past it a few times, landing once on the sandy beaches on its western shore. Rogers Island is protected land, dominated by a hardwood forest. In the understory grows an amazing array of plants, including, I have read, golden club.

These days, if I bought an island I could not name it for myself. In 1890 the United States Geological Survey standardized names and decreed that geographical features could not be named for living people. You have to be dead five years, and you must have had either a "direct and long-term association with the feature, or must have made notable civic contributions." The only place this does not hold true is in the Antarctic, where geographic features are named for people who are very much alive.

◊ ◊ ◊

The carriage road soon left solid ground and made its way through marshy lands. On either side of the causeway the water was swamplike, with bubbles of methane rising to the surface. Banded killifish swam in the slice of water near shore.

Looking into the marshy lands, I would have guessed I was in the Deep South and heading toward a bayou ringed with live oak and bald cypress, Spanish moss descending from their branches. I hopped on logs or skirted sections where puddles filled the causeway, telling me that the tide was going out. Reeds framed my walk, and honeysuckle was in bloom, as was honey locust, draping clusters of sweet-scented flowers. Yellow iris, introduced from Europe and the British Isles, bloomed. Its native cousin, blue flag, would follow soon with its purple blooms. It was almost unbearably lush.

I crossed the train tracks and brushed past grasses on my way toward the woods on Cruger Island. A sign warned me not to trespass and that the island was closed from January 1 until August 15. I assumed the ban was because of the eagle's nest. I hesitated for a moment, deciding whether to obey or ignore the sign. But for the health of an eagle I decided I could give up my golden club quest.

Disappointed, I turned around and walked back to a small wooden dock, where I sat to eat lunch. In front of me spatterdock, shiny new, emerged from the muck at low tide. By the end of the season I knew those same leaves would sport a coat of brown-gray silt. A stretch of mud fanned out in front of me, followed by a line of cattails from last year, the long brown cigar pods cracked, the reeds dry and brown. I called for my snappers. They were on the move that May. Already I had seen half a dozen crawling across land to lay their eggs.

To the west, the land rises where the train tracks run, and the embankment, except for a few underpasses, cuts off South and North Bays from the main river. After the tracks there is a gap, where the river flows, and then the layers mount, the small hills near the river, a few houses perched on top, then the higher layer, curving into the cut-out sky, of the Catskill Mountains. In the past few weeks they had begun to green, beginning at the bottom and working up, like a slow-motion paint job.

After lunch, I walked east toward campus. A ragged clearing in the woods lured me to explore. There, the ground undulates, dipping in an almost regular formation. At the end of a dip I uncovered a rectangular brass gravemarker about the size of a license plate. Who had been buried here in the woods? These were the graves of residents of a home for the aged that was established in Ward Manor, a large grey stone building a half mile down the carriage road. In 1926 William Boyd Ward, who owned a baking company, bought the house and donated it to the New York Association for Improving the Condition of the Poor. He turned over the operation of the house to William Matthews. Matthews created a welcoming place for poor people to spend the last years of their lives. Since 1963 Ward Manor has been a part of Bard College and now serves as a dorm.

I moved from one grave site to the next, uncovering the name plates that had been covered over with leaves and dirt.

Aiden Marcus Wakeman
Jan 24, 1867–Oct 15, 1947

Georgiana Egbert
Feb 20, 1868–Jan 17, 1957

Grace Percy Hazen
Oct 10, 1863–Feb. 23, 1954

Vandivere D. Moler
Aug 1, 1870–July 18, 1955

Minne Berggren
June 5, 1868–June 19, 1960

I could have spent all day—all week—cleaning off the markers. One after another, the names revealed themselves to me, but not the life stories. Who were these men and women who came to spend the final years of their lives in the old gray house? They were lost to history. I was trying to keep my parents alive by talking about them. But I realized that even with two people so loved, they too would soon be forgotten. Not by my sister or me, but by the larger world. I found that unbearable.

I turned north, dipping into the woods on the remains of a narrow asphalt road; then I climbed a steep hill to arrive on a flat open stretch. To the west the land is terraced, with fields flanking the woods. These fields were once farmed, also as part of Ward and Matthews's plan for the poor. In this area of the bays, they established four girls' camps.

It was in this same area in June 1997 that a thirty-four-year-old woman and her seven-year-old daughter were bound and raped. When I walk this land, I think of those two women then and now, the child no longer a child, their sadness and pain infinite. And, I wonder what happened to the man, who was never caught. Did he commit more crimes, poison more lives, and desecrate more land?

As an antidote to these thoughts, I like imagining the more distant past, the one full of children and summer fun. There's a wonderful treasure of photographs from this period donated by local residents, including Matthews's daughter, cataloged by Bard archivist Helene Tieger. Herds of smiling girls stand in front of quaint wooden buildings in one shot. Another photo shows a large group taking a ride on a hay wagon. Boys in bathing suits raft up the Hudson, which at the time was clear of water chestnut.

In Matthews's words, "The Boys' camp has its fun, its work, its discipline—the discipline that brings a freedom which comes from an acceptance of common control. Boys put on weight, acquire a coat of tan, learn a bit about trees, birds and frogs. Plain, common sense stuff about honor, trust-worthiness, of playing fair, of staying on the job—this too is mixed into the hours of play and work." The first summer of the camp, in the late 1920s, the boys built their own cabins on Cruger Island.

In this stretch of land, in addition to the girls' dorms, there were five "holiday bungalows," all with names of well-known New York hotels: Biltmore, Ritz, Plaza, Prince George, and Commodore. These rented at five dollars a week and were places where people from the city could vacation. There was a tennis court and a swimming pool, orchards and vegetable gardens. If I hadn't read about this past, I wouldn't have been able to see it in the grasses and trees that have reclaimed the land. How quickly a place is forgotten as well.

I continued north, and for the day I forgot about the elusive golden club. By the time I remembered to go and look again, their bloom would be over.

20

GRAVE SITES

Mary Burns stands about five feet four, with long dark-blond hair that she holds back in a thick ponytail. She is slight with wiry strong arms that she uses to speak. We first met on a Sunday morning at the Tivoli landing. Right away I was taken by her southern accent; her halting, precise manner of speech; and her quickness, both of mind and of laughter.

Mary had put out a call for volunteers to help her with a project on Magdalen Island. In a long e-mail she explained that she'd gotten a master of science in environmental studies from Bard College in 1998 and that her thesis involved "a study of, and stabilization plan for, a looted archeological site on the island." I did not understand what this meant. Still, I was curious, because the island Mary was working on lay within my reach. That meant it was *my* island, and if something was happening on it I wanted to know.

The island, just eight acres, is rich with over a dozen species of trees and looks like a primeval forest. One day in the spring, I wandered the western side of Magdalen, enjoying the musky smell where rocks—a mixed shale and sandstone called Greywacke—stack up like a sloppy deck of cards before disappearing into the deep water. When I reached the end of the island, I was focusing on the currents. But my eyes were drawn up to a bare branch. There, balanced at the top of a dead tree, was one of the biggest birds I had ever seen. Brown and white marked its long body. As I approached, it took flight, wings extended wide. An immature eagle. I continued to circle the island and saw that it had landed on a branch halfway up the island. I pulled back, not wanting to disturb it again.

The eagle made me feel like the island was a chosen place. But it wasn't just the eagle. It was also off of Magdalen that I had first heard a great blue heron taking flight at night, letting loose a hoarse *braak-ing* call. It was on the east side that I had seen thirty-two great egrets, shimmering dots reflecting white against the dark trees as they settled to roost for the night.

I had landed on the island only a handful of times. Once I had explored, locating a slab of rock on the western side that leans over, creating a soft, protected area. Walking the island, I saw used fire pits and informal paths that let me know that this wasn't my island. In fact, since 1985 it has been owned by the state. Day visitors are welcome, though signs warn against fires, camping, and digging. And yet people build fires, camp, and dig.

◊ ◊ ◊

Within minutes of introducing myself to Mary I said, "You think of it as your island, don't you?" We both laughed. I wondered how many other people thought of it as their island.

"It's fine," she said, "we can share Goat."

I smiled. Magdalen was originally named Slipsteen, then Goat, presumably because there were goats on the island. For the moment, we agreed to share the eight-acre treasure.

Mary struck out in her one-woman canoe, while I paddled next to her. After winding our way through the shallow, plant-choked waters, we beached on the still, east side of the island. We dragged our boats up high amidst mud and rocks and for good measure tied them to a tree. We tucked our pants into our socks in an attempt to keep ticks away, and sprayed for mosquitoes.

The tree-shaded entrance on the east side led me into Mary's world. I followed the path she had worn over the past fifteen years of visiting and working on the island. We stepped over downed branches and past bushes, up into the woods where she put down her box of photos, several maps, tape measures, and two bottles of water. As she prepared for our work, my eyes adjusted to the light that filtered through the high canopy.

"What are all the little pink flags?" I asked. Every twenty feet or so a small brightly colored plastic flag attached to a thin metal rod drooped two feet above the ground. There was no logic to their order, but there were lots of them, as if a surveyor had gone a bit berserk.

"Those are the looter pits."

"Each flag?"

Mary gave a smile that said she understood my disbelief, and that she shared it. "Each flag marks a different pit."

I stood for a long time, letting my vision travel deeper into the woods, through a clutter of trees and shrubs to where dozens of flags dotted the landscape.

"Oh my," I said, turning on my heels and looking through the leaves to see yet more flags.

A looter pit is a hole dug by someone looking, in this case, for Native American artifacts. They are not uniform round holes but rather amorphous indentations of various sizes. These were not small holes dug by a passing picnicker. These were holes dug by someone who knew what he or she was looking for. People had been looting the island since at least 1939. In eight-tenths of an acre on the eastern side Mary had identified over 200 pits. In every direction I could see tiny limp flags.

"Let me get this straight: you are identifying where things were?"

She nodded.

"You aren't looking for artifacts?"

"I'm not an archeologist," she said. "Most archeologists would not take on this site, damaged as it is."

So she was locating where artifacts had been, where someone had taken arrowheads, pottery, the story of a people. On a certain level I got it, why it was important to remember that people had lived here, though we would never know much about them. But on another level I was puzzled.

I had to ask again, "You're marking where people have dug?"

Mary was patient with me. No doubt she had been through this many times before. Since no westerner had ever built a house or camp on Magdalen, the island remains remarkably as it was thousands of years ago. For this reason alone Magdalen was a rich site. In 1939, Dr. Mary Butler from Vassar College conducted a survey in the Hudson Valley and found three sites on Magdalen: a shell midden, a rock shelter, and, where we stood, a seasonal campsite, which appeared to have been a workshop where Native Americans—either the Mohican from the east of the river to the north or the Delaware or Lenape groups from the west and south—made weapons and tools. Butler's work stopped when funding was cut during the war, but several more recent studies had moved forward, based on Butler's findings. All of these studies let us know that the artifacts on the island are—or were—significant. Mary had conducted her own study to find out that there is undisturbed soil amidst all of the digging. In the process she recovered tiny ecofacts—burned fish bone, nutshells, and seeds—all important clues to the past that can tell archeologists much about the subsistence strategies of the people who camped so long ago on this island.

Despite Butler's work and that of more recent archeologists, we had so little information about these Native people. And with each hole that I saw we had lost the possibility of learning more. Even if the looters handed over their treasures, the past could never be fully reclaimed. When artifacts are taken it is like "tearing pages from a book and scattering them around," Mary explained. The story is lost.

Lost stories. The idea made me desperate. I had journeyed to the southwest of France, and we had once again opened the family tomb. We did not have a service, did not gather people before the local priest. Rather, my sister, her two children and husband, and Odette and I stood holding hands and crying while the cheerful undertaker of the year before placed half of my father's ashes next to those of my mother and her mother. Our father's box of ashes was gray plastic, utterly practical next to the cream white urn of our mother. I worried then, still do now, that we should have bought a lovely container for him to rest in.

◊ ◊ ◊

Mary handed me a map on grid paper that she and a colleague had created using GPS and GIS. On this map were numbered dots, each one representing a looter pit. Each pit contained a yellow plastic disc with a corresponding number. Over the years the yellow plastic discs had been covered over with debris—leaves and dirt from erosion as well as decomposition. She wanted to locate all of them and replace them with numbered metal tags that preservationists in the future could find using a metal detector. With so many pits in such a small space, she was trying to impose order.

Keeping track of the pits, knowing what locations had been dug, would help Mary to know if there was any new digging. And, in the future, if technology changes—Mary imagines a time when we will be able to "look into" the soil without digging—we might easily see artifacts that remain in these dug sites.

In the past few days, with the help of other volunteers, she had located most of these yellow discs. Twenty remained elusive. She had highlighted those unfound dots. I looked at the markings on the map, dots that indicated where the treasure might once have been buried. I turned the paper to orient myself, to settle into the scale that translates the world onto a small, flat piece of paper. Then I walked a half dozen yards, following the grid, and estimated where the yellow plastic disc should be. *Could it be this easy?* I wondered. I crouched, my fingers playing in the dry brown leaves. Three inches down, my fingers grazed something hard and plastic. I pulled at the foreign texture, and out came a yellow disc about the size of the bottom of a good coffee mug. Dirt clung to the disc.

"You're good at this," Mary cheered.

"Call me Nancy Drew," I said, oddly intoxicated by my find. In a sense, finding the yellow plastic disc made me feel as if something remained in that empty pit.

Mary cackled, "OK, Nancy."

"Actually, you are the real Nancy Drew," I said. I stood up and brushed off my hands. "When was the last time you read Nancy Drew?" I mused. I had just reread the first in the series, *The Secret of the Old Clock.* "The opening of the first book explains why girls like me misunderstood what life was going to be," I told Mary. I recited the opening, which I had decided was important enough to memorize: "Nancy Drew, an attractive girl of eighteen, was driving home along a country road in her new, dark-blue convertible. She had just delivered legal papers for her father. 'It was sweet of Dad to give me this car for my birthday,' she thought. 'And it's fun to help him in his work.'" Our laughter echoed through the trees.

Throughout my life, I teased my father about the car he should buy me, that BMW or the Mercedes-Benz. But as much as my father loved to drive, he didn't pay much attention to cars, driving what fit him and was cheap enough to buy in cash—a VW bug, a Dodge Dart, a Fiat 128, and, later, a series of Mazdas. He was generous with food, wine, and his stories, but when it came to material things like cars, he balked. He made fun of the number of shoes I own. All that money I could have saved. Like many children of the Great Depression, my father lived as though he might have to grow another victory garden.

Imagining ourselves to be young sleuths, Mary and I spent the next four hours poking about the island, using a map and at times a measuring tape or photographs to help us locate the yellow tags. We brushed away leaves and sticks and tugged gently at the soil to find the markers of a world now gone.

As we worked, talking to coordinate where we thought we needed to sift through leaves, I had a sense of urgency and horror. Who had walked off with these treasures? At many of the pits brown beer bottles from a few decades ago lay empty. Soon they would become artifacts of a different sort. Nearby, tree roots had been hacked. Once the tree dies, the roots upend and the soil loosens, making the digging and taking easier. This was a mystery for Nancy Drew.

I watched Mary poke into the earth, energized by her work. Her focus was infectious. I no longer asked what we were doing but rather went along with this, certain her work mattered. At one point, I sat back on my haunches while Mary probed with a thin metal rod to find a tag. She wore a bandana across her forehead that caught the sweat before it trickled into her eyes.

I don't think it was just that I was awash in thoughts of death: the mounds of dirt surrounding me did look like simple grave sites, not unlike the grave sites of the old people who had lived in Ward Manor. The flags that hung above them were inadequate tributes to their scattered lives.

"This is heartbreaking business," I said.

Mary stopped for a moment. "Maybe I hitched my wagon to the wrong star, or whatever the expression is," she said. Her voice trailed off.

Or maybe she hadn't. What, though, would her work lead to? I didn't see any stars anywhere, and no fortune either. There had to be something, certainly not money, to explain her determination. Did she also spend long hours thinking about how quickly a life, a community, a world, vanishes? Maybe this was her way of fighting the inevitable.

Midafternoon, Mary led me to the rock shelter, the slanted piece of rock I had found on my own explorations. It is about twenty feet high and forty feet long, and now I knew it was a perfect place to camp—and has been for thousands of years. Mary broke up a fire circle, and we watched boats whiz by. From the vantage of Goat Island that water world I was usually a part of seemed far away and comparatively carefree.

I imagined the Native people standing at this spot, watching Hudson in his *Half Moon* moving north. Juet refers to the natives as the "people of the Countrey," and they come aboard the ship, bringing "greene Tobacco," as well as "Indian Wheat," and beaver skins, which Juet and his men "bought for trifles." Midjourney, near Albany, they "took them downe into the Cabbin, and gave them so much Wine and Aqua vitae, that they were all merrie." Throughout the journey, Juet writes that though the Natives "come in love," they "durst not trust them." There is perhaps some cause for wariness, as, after exploring Newark Bay and before heading up the river, one of the four Englishmen on board, John Colman, is killed with an arrow through his throat. And yet the trip north up the river is peaceful; it is the trip south when the violence begins. Some of the "people of the Mountaynes" come aboard and steal a "Pillow, and two Shirts and two Bandeleeres." One Native is shot, and soon another has his hands cut off by the cook. He drowns. The "Savages"—no longer the people of the country—swarm the boat, and several are shot.

Though Hudson showed sympathy toward the Natives he was unable to control his crew, who attacked with little cause (a stolen pillow?). And this crew was a violent one. On their voyage toward the New World they attacked a tribe of Mi'kmaq at LaHave in Nova Scotia, decimating a village. I wonder how different our history might be if these early explorers had come in peace.

As we returned to our work in the soaring heat, Mary stooped and picked up a piece of chert, the hard rock that breaks easily, creating sharp, cutting edges. This is what the Natives used to make their tools. It was tempting to take the chert home with me. In that desire I thought of what a thrill it would be to find an arrowhead. *Would I leave it where I had found it?* I wondered. I saw how the excitement of finding one object might lead to the next, might lead to digging. Could the simple rush of discovery explain the motives of the looters? Before we moved on, Mary replaced the chert where she'd found it.

We passed a sign tacked to a tree that warned against camping, fires, and digging.

"The signs don't do much, do they?"

Our laws are not equal to protecting the past. That is, the laws are both not rigid enough or enforced enough to protect these artifacts. There is the Archaeological Resources Protection Act (ARPA) of 1979. It offers solid protection to federal lands, where looting is a serious problem, particularly in the West. But on state lands such as Goat Island there was little anyone could do. If I walked into a person's house and admired their collection of arrowheads and asked where they got them they could say, "My backyard." And those arrowheads, and all that they can tell us about the past, belong to that person.

Who protects the dead? I thought of graveyards where pieces of tombs are taken, as souvenirs, perhaps, or acts of aggression. Tombs that hold family treasures, not just the bones and ashes of the dead, are ransacked. I knew no one would disturb my parents, resting in our family tomb in France. But I found the idea unsettling nonetheless.

We didn't stop our work until late in the afternoon, when the heat clobbered us. I was tempted to push on past dehydration because, in the past months, my ability to focus had slipped; distraction ruled. I was grateful for the day because for a stretch of time I had been focused on the one small, strange task that I had. We had found almost all of those yellow plastic discs. The sense of accomplishment gave me a sweaty satisfaction as we pushed off from the island.

◊ ◊ ◊

Over the next few weeks, I paddled south many times, short afternoon or evening outings where I looped around Goat Island. I looked for Mary's green canoe tied to a tree on the east side of her island. She was there every day, hours at a stretch. Her determination continued to puzzle and inspire me. A few times I saw her hugging the shoreline, making her way home after a day spent measuring and recording the loss. She always seemed a bit surprised to see me.

"I paddled around the island today," she reported by e-mail one night. "I wanted to see what you see."

What I see when I paddle around Goat is a small paradise. There is no sense from the water that the island has been torn and dug, has been violated. Then one day I stopped to visit the island alone. When I stepped out of my boat, I immediately felt spooked. The light on the island was dim, and a damp stillness took over. Was someone on the island, or were these the spirits of those who had lived there long ago?

As I followed Mary's faint trails, looking at the limp pink flags, an acorn dropped from a tree, pinging its way to the forest floor. Its landing rang in my ears. Adrenalin spun through my body. *Stay calm,* I told myself. Still, I could not leave fast enough. I am no Nancy Drew.

I wrote to Mary, asking her how she spent so many hours alone on the island. And she wrote back: "Were you out on our puffball?" That was the pet name she had given the island. "I often feel my hair is standing on end when I think a person I don't know might be walking around and it's just a squirrel! When you see me on the river canoeing home I'm almost in a daze from having been so on edge out there. Part of me loves the aloneness and part of me dreads it."

Love and dread. In that I understood what drew Mary to this work. Opposites generate energy. Energy is life. How much of my life, from those young camping trips at the dunes, had I lived twinning fear and exhilaration? I missed that. Sadness had so flattened my life that those vital tensions had all but vanished. I was no longer venturing out to scare myself on the river, had not paddled around Manhattan, and no longer slid out to skid across the dark, deep river at night. I could not bear to live in this state. *Il faut tenter de vivre.*

Commit life.

◊ ◊ ◊

I glided along in my boat, carving in near Goat Island. I could feel the sturgeon and striped bass below me. Overhead, I spied an eagle; a great blue heron took off near shore. The water was moving fast. I rocked my boat with my hips, gently at first, as if rocking a baby. And then I took a deep breath, tumbled over, fell out of my boat. I swam free into the turbid waters of my river.

21

SUMMER SOLSTICE

On the summer solstice I wanted to see the sun rise. I wanted to savor the longest day of the year, to absorb the tonic of sun and water. The weather had been painfully beautiful—clear, sunny, often with a breeze sweeping the sky clean. But I was so adrift that I could not make sense of these beautiful days. The solstice gave me reason to focus, to plan a long outing.

I awoke at 3:30 a.m. In the utter stillness I made coffee, and packed sunscreen, water, and my binoculars, which I had taken to using consistently. I wanted the world closer to me and in focus. I left the house at 4:15. It was 55 degrees out, and the first robins had begun their morning songs, calling the world to wake up.

Just out the driveway, I realized that I'd remembered my notebook, a bandana, and a hat but had forgotten food. On Broadway, just past the Methodist Church, I pulled over in front of the bakery. The front door was open. In a few hours, a row of people would be sitting on the bench on the porch, drinking coffee and eating buttery brioche and sticky buns. Every morning, while adults chatted on the porch sipping coffee, children played on the lawn in front of the bakery, chasing each other around the large silver maple tree.

When I asked Mikee the baker about that maple tree he told me that you need eighty gallons of sap from a silver maple tree to make one gallon of syrup. It only takes forty gallons of sap from a sugar maple tree. He is a baker who knows about a lot more than yeast and flour. If I need to know something, especially what is happening in Tivoli, I count on Mikee. He knows about weddings because he bakes the cakes, but he also knows about divorces, and affairs, and he was the first with information on the man who shot (but did not kill) his roommate in the trailer down on Montgomery Street. Mikee has opinions on everything, from the perfect olive oil to music to how to keep his bees happily producing honey. He also knows how to make a wonderful baguette. When the loaves are in the oven, the smell travels throughout the village. On those rare days when something burns, that smell travels as well.

Inside, the ovens hardly heated, I found Mikee in the back, his almost-white apron tied tight around his belly. He kissed me hello, our lips touching briefly. He did not act surprised to see me.

"What's fresh?" I asked. He peered at me over the tops of his wire-rimmed glasses and gestured to the two ovens, the empty racks, and the long metal table where the day's baking was in process. Obviously, nothing yet.

"There's day-old bread. And corn muffins." Mikee is not a baker who sells his day-old goods at half price. Anything less than fresh is less than perfect.

I buttered a chunk of the bread, grabbed a corn muffin studded with local, sweet strawberries, kissed Mikee good-bye, and was off. I wanted to be on the water before sunrise at 5:19.

At the landing, the water was still, and the darkness was both strange and familiar. I was on the other side of my nighttime paddles, during which darkness led into greater darkness. Here, I would be paddling toward light. Could I take that as a sign in my life? I wanted to. The first step was to play it out on the river.

A mist rose, the water warmer than the air. Out of the mist paddled a pair of mallard ducks that had lived at the Tivoli landing since spring. Looking at those ducks I thought of the miracle of couples. How was it I was incapable of what the ducks made look easy? And for forty-nine years my parents made it look easy as well. They traveled and did the crossword puzzle together, hosted parties and shared bottles of wine with contentment.

At this point I was romanticizing—openly and grandly—my parents' lives. My father would have objected. When he read my work he did not criticize poorly developed scenes or sloppy sentences. What he questioned was my allegiance to the truth. "It wasn't like this," he would say. Or, "Your mother isn't like that." I would insist on my version of the past, though often I should have deferred to his remarkable memory. Years after reading a novel he could describe characters and turns of plot with precision.

Now, I do not have to worry about his version standing against mine. He is not here to remind me how my mother's oncoming deafness tried his patience. Or how her desire to entertain had so often interrupted his writing. Or how her daily naps stunted many plans and outings. And she was not here to tell me how his obsession with the next meal drove her nuts, how she wished he would finish his latest novel. These irritations would, if I looked at it all honestly, let me know that the story was much more complex. Instead, I can remember as I please, become a child again, imagining that my parents' love for each other was pure and simple.

That, of course, wasn't even true for the ducks. It was odd this couple was still together; males usually leave after eggs are laid. I had seen them mating in the spring. It was a brutal affair: the male—in fact there were two males then—mounted her in a violent fury of feathers, fighting for the right to continue their genetic line. The female mallard sunk for so long I was sure she would drown. I was not being overly dramatic; some ducks do drown in the mating process.

"Don't you guys go somewhere at night?" I asked the ducks aloud. I saw their lives as precarious, living exposed through the dark.

At a bit before five, I pushed off. High tide was 7:30, so I had a couple of hours to paddle north, the current with me. A large cargo boat passed, pushed by a tug. I could see behind it two more barges. I wanted to cross the river but didn't dare venture out into the dark.

The boats cruised by in regular fifteen-minute intervals, their engines rattling the air and their wake making gentle long waves that lifted my kayak.

The western shore had already caught the first rays of sun and glowed a cerulean blue. The Catskills formed a crisp line. The eastern shore remained green-black, in a cold shade. My feet, wet from my entrance, were also cold. I moved in the shadow, waiting for the sun to pop over the ridge and warm me. It was a clear day, though the weather report called for possible afternoon thunderstorms.

Thirty minutes north, the long, graceful lawn that leads to the white Livingston home of Clermont emerged. Surrounding the home are magnolias that come into bloom in the spring, part of a wonderful assortment of trees. The tulip poplar puts out a bold orange tulip-shaped flower in June, just after the full white flowers of the catalpa tree. In late July the catalpa will produce long pods, like overgrown green beans, which mature in the fall.

Finally the sun snuck over the eastern ridge and lapped over me. I slipped on my sunglasses and pulled down my hat. So quickly the texture of the air shifted. The thrum of dawn was on. I stuck to the eastern shore, moving with the current past the Carmelite sisters in their brick dormitory-style building. Several beautiful houses, most former Livingston properties, sat dark and quiet with sleep. As I approached the landing at Cheviot I noted that the Upper Flats, which at low tide reveal grass and spatterdock, were submerged. In the fall on these flats, hunters slap up wooden blinds and wait for the ducks to arrive on their migration south.

The landing at Cheviot is a sloping cement loading dock used by those easing their motorboats into the water. I settled into a picnic table near the edge of the landing and unpacked my buttered bread and a thermos of coffee. Mikee's bread, even a day old, had a crisp crust and was soft inside. It smelled yeasty and tasted like heaven.

Just off of Cheviot is a tiny island with a few ragged trees. In the past I had seen cormorants draped over the island, their black wings spread to dry in the breeze. I had taken the ungainly black cormorants for granted. But I'd seen few this summer. I missed them. In the news there were reports that cormorants were so numerous they were being blamed for the decline in sport fisheries. It's hard to believe, but as a scapegoat, the cormorant is a good one. With their shiny black coats and long necks that appear snakelike in the water, they are ominous looking.

Across the river, in Greene County, a new house, octagonal with glass walls (Fowler's enduring influence?), showed growth in sleepy Smith's Landing. Until recently, the town was named Cementon. In hopes of changing their cement-based image, local residents reverted to the town's original name of Smith's Landing. Cementon does conjure up a company town with a saloon and rough men covered in dust. This is the truth of Cementon, as in 1910 the town had fourteen saloons. Brawls and gunfights were subjects for the local papers. At the turn of the twentieth century, Cementon was home to three cement plants. Two of those plants—the ones I could see from Cheviot—are still in use.

Several times I had put in at Cheviot at night, the lights at the factories on the far shore speckling green and white. It was beautiful. In Edith Wharton's novel *Hudson River Bracketed*, one of the wealthy landowners says: "The world's simply dying of a surfeit of scenery—an orgy of beauty. If my father would cut down some of the completely superfluous trees, and let us get a line on the chimney of the cement factory. . . . It's a poor little chimney, of course, but it's got the supreme qualities of ugliness." And in their ugliness they become beautiful. Especially at night.

A slim man walked up. He moved quickly, as if agitated. His jeans needed a good washing; tattoos festooned his arms. I recognized his face, had seen him around Tivoli. But I didn't want to see him there at six in the morning on a desolate dock.

I expected him to be like others I've met on the river, a bit aloof, staring at his reach of the river. At almost every landing along the river I found men sitting in cars, taking time from work or home to be by the water. Initially, these waterside lurkers made me a bit nervous. Now, I had come to expect them.

The man straddled the other side of the picnic table from me. "I'm Jack," he said stretching out a hand to shake. His hand was strong and rough. He lived with his girlfriend, Sarah—he referred to her as "my Sarah"—and together they had renovated her house. He pointed east, across the train tracks and up the steep hill where houses cling to the narrow road. The house with the porch was his. He told me what they paid for the house and for the renovation, half of what a contractor estimated. In the process he had had a nervous breakdown. Since I was midrenovation of my kitchen I understood how dust and stray nails hold no charm, how the sound of a circular saw works its way back behind the eyes, and how going forward requires an ability to see the future, clean and insulated. And I knew how, some days, an empty checking account squashed that vision.

"Ended up in the VA hospital," he said motioning his head north, toward Albany.

"Where did you serve?" I asked.

"Beirut, 1983. There wasn't a war. But still. If people tell you they aren't afraid, they're lying."

I nodded.

He told me about fishing off Cheviot, and how one day he hooked a fish that started towing his boat—he cut the line. "People make fun of me, but I had 650 pounds of gear and people in that boat." He shook his head. "Had to be a sturgeon."

I asked what had happened to the cormorants.

"An eagle is nesting on the island. Scared them off."

I looked to the lopsided tree on the island, certain an eagle nest would be visible.

Jack, jangly, as if he'd drunk a pot of coffee, told me about a kid who ran his boat up on the rocks that emerge at low tide between land and the island. "Took out the bottom of the boat." We both laughed.

War stories, fishing stories, boating stories, home improvement stories—all in twenty minutes. Jack's cell phone rang. His Sarah wanted to know whom he was talking to. I waved toward the house up the hill, got up, and slid my boat back into the water.

I continued north, hugging the shoreline and reveling in the lushness of summer growth. I was now firmly out of my reach, and I realized how I had not yet wandered from it that summer. The weight of melancholy had made me stay in the familiar, inclined me to risk less.

Moving north into terrain I knew, but not well, left me feeling a bit exposed.

Yet this trip felt right. As the sun began to warm my back, the anxiety that was driving me started to loosen. Since my father's death I woke several times each night, unsure of where I was. But it wasn't just at night that I was disoriented. What I had come to realize was that I had organized myself around my parents, and in the past year and a half I had focused on my father. While we were in Arizona our daily life was lovely and compatible. I have rarely been as happy as I was those peaceful two weeks in the desert. What I had discovered mid-age is the contentment of companionship, how loneliness is tempered by sitting near, or sharing a meal with, someone I love. I was treating it as a grand discovery, but most people seem to get it without having to wake up at 3:30 in the morning and throw themselves onto the Hudson River.

When I bought my house, all of the paperwork, inspections, and lawyer visits seemed complicated. Every house I would pass made me think: *Someone owns that house. They went through all the steps I am going through. If they can do it, so can I.* Now, I looked at all of my friends, coupled in their various ways, and thought: *If they can do it, so can I.* But could I?

I was forty-six years old and bobbing about in my life without children, parents, spouse or partner. The sensation was one of drifting. I hated it. And so I pushed myself through each day, keeping myself more busy than necessary. Movement helped. It always did. On land it was a flight from feeling. On the river the paddling let me settle into what I felt, let me live with the pain, without fear of where that would take me. I had to take the next stroke. The simple necessity of that kept me afloat.

◊ ◊ ◊

The eastern shore above Germantown remains undeveloped except for a few houses and a large brick building with Germantown Cold Storage written on it. I landed at North Germantown sooner than expected. Coasting into the cement loading dock, I tugged myself out of my boat. Still in my yellow life vest with my spray skirt, an ugly black apron, dangling down to my knees, I walked past the large cottonwood trees and onto the wooden floating dock that extends into the water. North, the river opens up, then vanishes as it curves slightly west. Across the river, at Long Point, broods a cement plant. It has six hoppers that resemble grain silos with long arms sticking straight out.

The peaceful landing tempted me to stay. But I wanted to see how far I could ride the current north. And on this venture I had the sense that my spirits were returning in installments as I passed through reach after reach.

Every time I've paddled north of Germantown the wind kicks up. Waves knock me around and I end up feeling beaten by the elements. Today I hoped for calm as I crossed the river, scanning north and south. I tucked into Embought Bay (sometimes spelled Inbocht Bay), which yawns open to the river, slow and dense with water chestnut.

On a log, stilled in the bay, lounged an enormous snapping turtle, sunning its spacious back. I floated closer to offer the turtle my respects; with one shove of its legs it flopped into the water and vanished. An osprey flapped by overhead, scanning the water for its next meal. A heron stood statuesque amongst the water chestnut. Out on the river, on marker I I I, which flashes green every four seconds, cormorants clustered. I was happy to see them.

Two twiggy nests shared a platform high above the water. I pulled out my binoculars and strained to see fuzzy cormorant heads sticking out. But I saw nothing. What was apparent, though, was that the nests weren't just twigs. There was also string and other man-made materials, like the plastic rings that hold soda cans, laced in. Ospreys make chaotic nests as well, only bigger. Having a nest in direct sunlight seemed a bad idea, but the parents carry water in their beaks to douse and cool off the young.

I loitered near the bay, enjoying all the sights. Then I realized that I was being pushed south with the current. At nine, the current had changed its course. And the wind was against me. I had no interest in struggle. I did not need to be knocked around by the river.

On my return I stuck to the western shore, which I'd never paddled before. There's a reason for that. The series of cement plants that edge the water have deep channels that run next to them so that barges can

sidle up and take on or discharge loads. This means that I was paddling in the shipping lane. Nervous, I twisted in my seat to look back,
scanning for a boat that might bear down on me. I scooched into the
channel as I passed Long Point, where a barge floated at anchor next
to large cement silos. When I had looked at the barge and plant from
North Germantown on the eastern bank, I thought it all a fantastic
sight. Now, hugging close to the side of the barge, I was edged with
worry. It towered above me, the force of its steel flanks palpable.
I doubted anyone on board saw me there, low in the water.

Cement is one of the few remaining industries in the valley, with
three factories on the Hudson south of Albany. Cement in the Hudson Valley was, in the 1800s, a mainstay, and more was produced here
than anywhere else in the country. Most of New York City was built
from Hudson Valley cement, much of it a natural cement. The cement industry now produces Portland cement, which is a mixture of
clay and limestone. This Portland cement is less strong but sets more
quickly.

In recent years St. Lawrence Cement tried to expand its production by building a 353-million-dollar coal-fired plant in the city of
Hudson. It met with powerful resistance. Unlikely allegiances were
forged between the arts, gay, and other local communities to keep the
plant away. After six years of battle, the plans were turned down by
the New York State Department of State. It was a stunning moment,
chronicled in a sharp documentary, *Two Square Miles.* What the DOS
voted against is less important than what it was voting for: the scenic,
historic, and recreational use of the river and valley. It was voting for
me to be there in my kayak floating on the Hudson on the morning
of June 21.

◊ ◊ ◊

The western shore is scalloped, each point echoed by a cove. While
the points are developed, the coves, surrounded by shallow water, are
undeveloped forests. Past Long Point, Duck Cove lured me in before
I looped out to Silver Point, where another barge was tied up at the

dock next to six cement silos. Again, I shimmied by as fast as possible. The captain stood in his glass-encased deckhouse and waved to me.

Near Eve's Point a pair of bald eagles sat high in a tree, fluffing their feathers in the sun. Regal and calm, they ignored me loitering below them, watching through my binoculars.

The summer of 2007, the bald eagle was taken off the endangered species list. From a low of 410 breeding pairs in the 1960s to around 10,000 now they have experienced a remarkable comeback. The situation in New York State was dire in the 1970s—there was one breeding pair. It was not until 1997 that a breeding pair settled in the Hudson Valley. These birds in the vicinity of Eve's Point were a part of this repopulation. Through the summer, I saw more and more eagles—it's an untrained birder's dream because they are a bit hard to miss. Each sighting felt magical all the same. Seeing these eagles, I thought again of couples. The mallard ducks. Jack with his Sarah. My parents.

Was it in coupling that creatures found themselves tied to this world? Did the eagles survive not just out of an urgent biological imperative but also because of and for one another? Would a lone eagle more likely die, exposed in the world? Maybe, but it would not die of loneliness, and neither would I. I had reached a new low, using bald eagles to indulge my self-pity. "Snap out of it," my father would say.

I pulled onto shore to drink the last of my coffee. A dead fish, covered in flies, marinated in the sun. I stepped downwind of it. And then, suddenly, I remembered my promise to Edie, a writer friend, to walk with her that day as distraction and for good health as she waited for her second baby to emerge into the world. I pulled out my cell phone.

"I'm at Stewart's," she said, her voice echoing through the phone.

"I'm on the river paddling," I said, enjoying the contrast between where she was and where I sat. Stewart's was a local convenience store, which smelled of stale coffee and hot dogs left too long to cook.

"I'm going into labor," Edie said.

"In Stewart's?" That was all wrong.

"I'm in the bathroom."

"Get out of there, Edie," I said.

◊ ◊ ◊

In 1979 my father wrote an essay titled "Nature, Books, Yaddo, Tolstoy, Life and Art." The essay is just what the title indicates—it's that rambling—and was written for me while my father was visiting the artist colony Yaddo. I was in Colorado, climbing in Eldorado Canyon. I had taken *War and Peace* with me and in a letter to him had announced I had read all of fifteen pages. In the essay, he meditates on the intersection of the natural world with the world of art, or, to put it another way, the yearning for a simple, natural life, and the pull of the spiritual, complicated world of art. He had that pull to a more simple life, a life where his mind was less active, perhaps even less, as I said as an adolescent, weird. Reflecting on himself in the third person, my father saw himself in me: "She, too, had the longing to be simple and natural and uncomplicated and perhaps she had a better chance of achieving such a state of being than he had ever had. Though could anyone achieve it? He wondered. Was simplicity possible?"

I didn't think it was. There is no such thing as a simple relationship or a simple house purchase. There is not a simple rock climb or a simple river to paddle on. Wanting any of it to be simple had been my mistake. The river had taught me to embrace the complexity of the undeveloped coves shadowing the cement factories. I now was translating that truth to other parts of my life. I was, as I had hoped, paddling toward light.

From where I sat by the river, the eagles perched nearby, it was all so peaceful, so beautiful. Simply beautiful.

◊ ◊ ◊

I pointed surely south, paddling without energy, coasting with the current. Heat splashed up as I crossed over after the Saugerties Lighthouse. When I pulled out of the water it was one in the afternoon.

I had been on the river for eight hours, and the day felt complete—and as if it were just beginning. Perhaps there was new life beginning. I pulled out my cell phone and called Edie, only to go directly to voicemail. Was she safe at the birthing center? I would learn soon that she was, with a new baby girl.

I looked into the rest of the day, the rest of the summer. Anything might happen. But at that moment there was nothing as glorious as the turtle or the eagles, nothing as affirming as the pair of ducks or the nesting cormorants, nothing as simple and purposeful as each paddle stroke, nothing as sure as the movement of the river.

22

LOVE FOR A RIVER

I pulled down Foster Avenue in State College expecting to find my father, pants dirty, stooped over his flowers, insisting I come look at the latest bloom. But what I found was a stilled house. As I walked room to room it appeared already empty. That was what I had to do: empty the house, take apart the history of our family, closet by closet, drawer by drawer.

For a short time I considered moving back to this place I often still referred to as home. But I knew I could not move back, even though losing the house meant losing the town, my past. This saddened me beyond what I could have imagined. And so anticipating the change, I came to love State College in a whole new way. Every time I met someone I knew while running errands downtown I was delighted. There was my English teacher from high school, who I will always think of as Mrs. Spanier, now a Hemingway scholar at the university, and Geoff, the owner of Appalachian Outdoor House—still in business—who taught me to rock climb back in 1975. Walking the downtown I remembered when the building where the bank—Peoples

National Bank—now stands was People's Nation, a store that sold bongs, lava lamps, and waterbeds. And one night, while attending a play in a downtown theater, I realized the lobby was where Danks had been, the place I bought my first white, padded bra. These memories were small but seemed so important. They were like the memories my neighbor Ann had of making egg creams at the candy store in downtown Tivoli. These small-place memories are becoming rare in a world where we all move so easily.

In Tivoli I had known the Morey, which locals called Bayly's, a bar that was only for locals, and a bit run-down. I had walked past the empty schoolhouse before it was renovated into apartments. There was a sapling growing through the roof of the Methodist Church before the slates were removed and the spire rebuilt one cold winter. But these memories ran only so deep. I didn't have memories like Helene Tieger, who grew up in Tivoli. She remembers the candy store: "You could buy a week's worth of Swedish Fish, Dots, Mary Janes, and FireBalls with the dollar your grandmother pressed into your hand," she told me. "The candy store was also referred to as Moore's. Later it was owned by Stan and Doris Williams." For Helene, Stan and Doris have faces and personalities; to me they are names from the past.

My deepest memories would remain in central Pennsylvania. State College would always be my home. But not one Rogers was going to be buried in State College—we had come and stayed, but we wouldn't stay forever. So now, the longest relationship I would ever have to a place was about to end.

In late August, Becky flew in from France, and for ten days we hauled 2.4 tons of stuff—old beds and broken chairs—from the attic or basement and heaved them into a metal dumpster installed in the driveway. On the first weekend of our work, the doorbell rang, and there on the doorstep stood Phil Doucette, a friend from high school. He had read about our father's death in the newspaper and had come to the funeral. Here he was to help clean out the house. He called others to help us as well: Paul Hester and Joe Gerstner, my sister's high-school boyfriend. It took us both a few beats to recognize Joe with a beard and a few wrinkles. We had played flashlight tag in the park with these men, wrestled through adolescence. Now here we were adults, with some marriages, relationships, affairs, divorces, and children among us. We had a lot to catch up on, but more importantly, we had a house to empty. We put them to work—lifting boxes, vacuuming the attic and basement, fixing the plumbing in the downstairs bathroom. They were heroic.

One downside of having a writer as a father: he had about 10,000 books, several drafts of the four novels he had written, and had saved every letter sent to our family, organized in five four-drawer filing cabinets in the basement. I found it hard to just whiz through any drawer; I stopped to scan, to dip into words and moments from the past. My father kept everything, from his grade-school drawings (as well as Becky's and mine) to the first three-cent piece his grandfather earned, a dollar bill from 1863, and lots and lots of photographs.

The hardest trips to State College were when I was alone, sorting and tossing without Becky to consult. We thought we knew the contents of every drawer, and then I'd find new treasures: my father's letters from Alaska, when he was stationed there in 1946. Or his letters home from Europe in 1950. Every day Becky would call to check on my progress, and, no matter how dusty and tired I was, we would end up laughing.

But I was never long alone in the house. Across the street, Ron and Sandy cooked lasagna, mixed martinis in memory of my father, and poured glasses of wine. The Rambeaus invited me for coffee in the morning. Manya shared half-price burgers at Duffy's Tavern, carrying on my father's Monday night tradition. And on Saturday mornings through the summer and fall I joined a group of neighbors who gathered to weed and mulch in the fantastic, perhaps excessive garden that wraps around the house. They called themselves the Garden Brigade, though there were only a few true gardeners among them. They are smart, busy people, who had their reasons to gather and pull weeds in the garden of a man who had just died.

"I did not hear enough of your father's stories," Bill wrote to me. "This is what I can do."

Back in Tivoli, I also gardened. I got my gardening habits—the whimsy of it, the chaos of it—from my father. Behind the house I had carved a circular flower bed, reserved for plants I would bring from his garden. I had already taken rhubarb and a daylily, which was struggling to orient itself in the Tivoli clay soil. This soil was great for the brick industry but not so good for my flowers. I had added bags of peat moss and organic soil. I had been composting for years, digging in the dark compound to make the soil richer. Through digging and mixing, I now had several feet of good growing soil.

With each layer that I added to the soil, I saw how I was making this place home, was anchoring myself to this little patch of Tivoli. Without my parents as my anchor in this world, I needed to create my own secure spot, I needed to be kept safe.

When people walking the quiet of Feroe Avenue stopped to admire my flowers they heard of my father—that he just died, that he was a gardener, that this flower had been his. I could not keep myself from speaking about him.

On a Monday evening, I was spreading mulch in the strip of garden by the driveway when a woman biked past and waved. "Hi, it's Natalie," she said. We had met at our local Japanese restaurant, a week or so earlier, and had a handful of friends in common. I waved at Natalie, so cheerful on her bike in the evening air.

When I came in from gardening, I found a phone message from Natalie inviting me over to her house, which is perched above the Hudson River. Since I had never been in one of the houses that looms above my reach, I said yes. I bicycled over, my headlamp barely piercing the darkness. Natalie was outside, staring at the wonders of the world, Venus bright in the sky. Taken by the dark and the blinking fireflies, we walked out a path mowed into the vast lawn. The lights of Saugerties studded the far shore, and the low hum of traffic on the New York State Thruway, which I never hear on the river, was audible high up.

As we walked I realized that this was where Dorothy Day had walked. This piece of land once belonged to the acres that made up her Catholic Worker Farm. The main house, Rose Hill, was just down the hill from Natalie's modern house.

What advice would Day give to me? Find friends, make community. Learn to commit to more than the next paddle stroke. Throw down an anchor into the clay soil on which you have spread your mulch. Make that choice and stick to it.

We approached the woods, and an animal began a howl of utter, heartbroken sorrow. It was the cry of a mother whose young are being taken. It was the sound Becky and I made, me lying on my floor in Tivoli and she in France, the phone line joining our cries of despair when I called and announced, "Papa is dead."

Natalie and I froze in the path, wanting the sound to stop. But all we could do was listen.

"Cup your ears; you can hear it louder."

I cupped my ears but couldn't bear it. After what seemed an eternity—a minute—the sound stopped, suddenly, without a whimper or trailing off. Done. Had a coyote or a fox taken the life of some small animal? We would never know.

We walked back, more quickly than we'd walked out, into the safety of Natalie's neat home. We drank tea at her kitchen table, and then she played songs she had just recorded, children's poems, so seemingly innocent, sung in a melodious, sexy voice. If I did not garden I never would have heard any of the sounds—the cries or the songs—I heard that night.

Over the next few weeks, with her husband and daughter visiting family in Spain, Natalie was free to play. She would call and say, "I'm stir-crazy; let's go for a bike ride." We referred to the shaded ride up Woods Road as the womb, because it felt safe, protected from the world. And because in the womb wonderful things happened. One day a barred owl swooped across the road, landed, and stared down at us until we could no longer stare back. Another day we found a snapping turtle crossing Woods Road. She was huge, like a broken gray-brown serving plate. I wanted to touch her, to feel her shell to see how soft or hard it is, but the stories of how these animals can extend their long necks and swing around for a snap kept me at a distance. Her slow-motion movement on fleshy, elephantine legs, each one clawing forward one small step at a time, gave us long minutes to admire the tenacity of this creature. There was something both serious and cheerful about her movement, a real role model. While she made her way across the road, Natalie and I directed cars to slow and make a loop around our treasure.

Together, Natalie and I had a pool of knowledge about the area and the houses that were hidden by the woods, the same houses that

I saw from the river. Down one driveway lived a celebrity, and down another was a Livingston heir. Another house was Oak Hall, where Eleanor Roosevelt spent much of her childhood with aunts and uncles. Always, we were tempted to cycle in to visit the Carmelite sisters on their vast property overlooking the river.

Together we explored the back roads of Columbia County, detouring to pass the farm that kept bison, emu, and elk. Further up the road, we agreed on the perfect farmhouse, the one with the goats and ducks and an elaborate herb garden. We stopped in graveyards and wandered, reading the names of people we would never know. We picked blueberries and peaches. We referred to these golden weeks as Camp Tivoli.

One night Natalie wanted to bike, but I was set on a paddle. Without hesitation, she wanted to join me. On the river, she took her paddle and scooped into the water. When I told her to lean into her turns she did, grazing near the water. I laughed at her fearlessness and energy. We slipped down to Magdalen Island, the river becoming ever darker. Then, as we surged north, toward home, Natalie made loud whooping noises, her voice echoing off the shore. I joined her, chanting along. We were the "people of the country," and this was our land.

We pulled onto shore, and left our boats rocking in the small waves. Natalie turned to the water, waded out hip deep, then plunged in. I joined her, swimming out until we could no longer touch bottom. Together, we splashed in the warm summer water. I showed her the one-finger sidestroke, then the short man's backstroke, which I had learned from my father.

On Natalie's long dirt driveway, lined with pin oak and chestnut trees, we stopped the car and got out. The open field was alive with fireflies. We stood entranced, as she told me about her first boyfriend, and I told her about mine. In different ways, we had both feared ending up pregnant as teenagers. Now I wished for those babies I had so dreaded.

I wanted to be able to say *mine*: my child, my spouse, my house, my garden. My reach. In staking my claims, I was showing my love. But also, I was making my choices, just as Day had made hers. And those choices would anchor me to this world.

The fireflies increased as we watched, swarming above the open field. It was beautiful, the dots of light hallucinatory. We walked to a marshy area, the display so hypnotic we stood for an hour, watching the lights flicker.

Camp Tivoli made me believe I was young again, could start over, with all the world and life in front of me. What would I do differently? Nothing. Because it all led up to that moment, watching the fireflies over the marsh and talking about the difficulty and necessity of love.

What anchored me to this world? Love for my sister and her two children, love for my parents, love for my friends, love for the river.

By now I knew, of course, that if I loved the river, the river was indifferent to me. Still, the river had carried me through the past two years of loss and sadness. Its waters had offered up sights and smells, creatures large and small, to distract and delight me. It had offered up its watery belly as a place to explore and hide, a place to find these stories.

Dizzy with the fireflies, I weaved my way home.

BOOKS CONSULTED

In writing this book I relied a great deal on two titles:

Boyle, Robert. *The Hudson River: A Natural and Unnatural History.* New York: Norton, 1969.

Carmer, Carl. *The Hudson.* New York: Holt, Rinehart and Winston, 1939.

I read and consulted many other works in the course of writing this narrative:

Adams, Arthur G. *The Hudson River Guidebook.* 2nd ed. New York: Fordham University Press, 1981.

——. *The Hudson River in Literature: An Anthology.* Albany: State University of New York Press, 1980.

Burns, Mary. "Goat Island." Talk delivered as part of the Department of Environmental Conservation Tivoli Bay Talks, June 4, 2009.

Burroughs, John. *The Heart of Burroughs's Journals.* Boston and New York: Houghton Mifflin, 1928.

——. *A River View and Other Hudson Valley Essays.* Selected and introduced by Edward Renehan. Croton-on-Hudson, NY: North River Press, 1981.

Carr, Archie. *Handbook of Turtles.* Ithaca, NY, and London: Comstock Publishing Associates, 1952.

Cronin, John, and Robert F. Kennedy, Jr. *The Riverkeepers: Two Activists Fight to Reclaim Our Environment as a Basic Human Right.* New York: Scribner, 1997.

Crowley, Jim. *Lighthouses of New York: Greater New York Harbor, Hudson River, and Long Island.* Saugerties, NY: Hope Farm Press, 2000.

Day, Dorothy. *The Eleventh Virgin.* New York: Albert and Charles Boni, 1924.

——. *The Long Loneliness: An Autobiography.* New York: Harper & Row, 1952.

——. *On Pilgrimage.* Grand Rapids, MI: William B. Eerdmans Publishing Company, 1999. First published 1948 by Catholic Worker Books.

Department of Environmental Conservation. "Juvenile Atlantic Sturgeon Sonic Tracking Project." http://www.dec.ny.gov/animals/9968.html.

DuLong, Jessica. *My River Chronicles: Rediscovering America on the Hudson.* New York: Free Press, 2009.

Dunwell, Frances F. *The Hudson: America's River.* New York: Columbia University Press, 2008.

——. *The Hudson River Highlands.* New York: Columbia University Press, 1991.

Giddy, Ian H., and the Hudson River Watertrail Association. *The Hudson River Water Trail Guide.* 6th ed. New York: Hudson River Watertrail Association, 2003.

Huler, Scott. *Defining the Wind: The Beaufort Scale and How a 19th-Century Admiral Turned Science into Poetry.* New York: Crown, 2007.

Hummel, Meredith, and Stuart Findlay. "Effects of Water Chestnut (*Trapa natans*) Beds on Water Chemistry in the Tidal Freshwater Hudson River." *Hydrobiologia* 559 (2006): 169–81.

Hunter, Douglas. *Half Moon: Henry Hudson and the Voyage That Redrew the Map of the New World.* New York: Bloomsbury Press, 2009.

Juet, Robert. *Juet's Journal of Hudson's 1609 Voyage from the 1625 Edition of Purchas His Pilgrims.* Transcribed by Brea Barthel. www.halfmoonreplica.org/Juets-journal.pdf.

Keene, Carolyn. *The Secret of the Old Clock.* New York: Grosset & Dunlap, 1930.

Kiviat, Erik. "A Hudson River Tidemarsh Snapping Turtle Population." *Transactions of the Northeast Section, The Wildlife Society* 37 (1980): 158–68.

——. "Loosestrife: Purple Peril or Purple Prose?" *Hudsonia* 14, no. 2 (1999): 158–68.

Kiviat, Esther. *Changing Tides: Tivoli Bays; A Hudson River Wetland.* Fleischmanns, NY: Purple Mountain Press, 1999.

Levinton, Jeffrey S., and John R. Waldman, eds. *The Hudson River Estuary.* New York: Cambridge University Press, 2006.

Lewis, Tom. *The Hudson: A History.* New Haven, CT: Yale University Press, 2005.

Lourie, Peter. *River of Mountains: A Canoe Journey down the Hudson.* Syracuse, NY: Syracuse University Press, 1995.

Marranca, Bonnie. *A Hudson Valley Reader: Writings from the 17th Century to the Present.* Woodstock, NY: The Overlook Press, 1995.

Matthews, William H. *In and About a Grey Stone Manor House.* New York: AICP, 1929.

Moore, Lela. *A Brief History of Tivoli.* Self-published, 1921.

Mylod, John. *Biography of a River: The People and Legends of the Hudson Valley.* New York: Hawthorn Books, 1969.

Navins, Joan. *Tivoli: 1872–1972.* Rhinebeck, NY: Jator Printing, 1972.

Richardson, Judith. *Possessions: The History and Uses of Haunting in the Hudson Valley.* Cambridge, MA: Harvard University Press, 2003.

Rinaldi, Thomas E., and Rober J. Yassinsac. *Hudson Valley Ruins.* Lebanon, NH: University Press of New England, 2006.

Rombauer, Irma S., Marion Rombauer Becker, and Ethan Becker. *Joy of Cooking.* New York: Scribner, 1931.

Ruttenber, E. M. *Indian Tribes of Hudson's River to 1700.* Saugerties, NY: Hope Farm Press, 1992.

Stanne, Stephen P., Roger G. Panetta, and Brian E. Forist. *The Hudson: An Illustrated Guide to the Living River.* New Brunswick, NJ: Rutgers University Press, 1996.

Stone, Ward B., Erik Kiviat, and Stanley A. Butkas. "Toxicants in Snapping Turtles." *New York Fish and Game Journal* 27, no. 1 (January 1980): 39–50.

Teale, Edwin Way. *The Lost Woods.* New York: Dodd, Mead & Co, 1946.

Van Zandt, Roland. *Chronicles of the Hudson.* Hensonville, NY: Blackdome Press, 1992.

Wharton, Edith. *Hudson River Bracketed.* New York: Appleton & Co, 1929.

Wiles, Richard C. *Tivoli Revisited: A Social History.* Rhinebeck, NY: Moran Printing, 1981.

Willis, Nathaniel Parker. *Out-Doors at Idlewild; or, The Shaping of a Home on the Banks of the Hudson.* New York: Scribner, 1855.

ACKNOWLEDGMENTS

Several chapters from this narrative were previously published in different forms, and I would like to thank the editors of the journals in which earlier versions of those chapters appeared. Chapter 3 first appeared as "Swimming the River" in *Stone Canoe: A Journal of Arts and Ideas from Upstate New York*, no. 5, Spring 2011; chapter 11 as "Solace of a Dark, Wide River" in *Under the Sun*; chapter 13 as "If You Are Lucky" in *Isotope: A Journal of Literary Nature and Science Writing* (Spring/Summer 2009); and chapter 18 as "Sitting by the River" in *Alaska Quarterly Review* 27 (Fall/Winter 2010).

I have many people to thank.

Boyer Rickel and Donna Steiner both read this manuscript more times than is reasonable to expect of any friend. I will be forever grateful.

Those who appear in this book and shared in my adventures—Emmet Van Dreische, Sarit Shatken, Carrie and Emily Majer, Carol Lewis, Natalie Merchant, Dawes Strickler, Sue Kligerman, Mary

Burns, and John Cronin. John taught me much about the river; his wisdom and encouragement are at the heart of this book.

Many wonderful colleagues at Bard College—really too many to list!—and especially Leon Botstein, president of the college, kept me focused and energized. Bard College sustained me in many ways and gave me time to write as well as financial assistance. Through the years, my students at Bard have inspired me with their lives and their words.

I turned to the smart and critical eye and encouragement of many readers, including BK Loren, Michael Ives, Erica Kiesewetter, Mary Caponegro, cousin Lisa Redburn, and my partner in off-river adventures, Teri Condon.

My State College family will remain my first true home. To the Garden Brigade: the spirit of our Saturday morning weed-pulls makes me smile. It takes neighbors to keep a garden.

To the village of Tivoli: I couldn't imagine a finer place to call home.

My colleagues of River Summer 2005: I learned much from you and from living on a boat.

Luc Sante and Edie Meidav offered generous words as the manuscript first sailed into the world. Eric Lind at Audubon, Julia Wentzel, and Liza Birnbaum gave their keen eyes and technical expertise to improve this book. Helene Tieger shared her local knowledge, which runs deep into the history of Tivoli and of Bard. Erik Kiviat at Hudsonia was generous with his knowledge, both local and scientific, of Tivoli Bay and fed me a healthy diet of reading material, particularly on turtles. John Lipscomb at Riverkeeper and Sasha Pearl at the Saugerties Lighthouse offered me insightful and often entertaining stories about the river. Robert Kelly and Charlotte Mandell helped with translation and were there with teapots of encouragement. Linda Gruntwagin at the post office blessed my manuscript as it went into the world.

Jessica DuLong slipped my manuscript to Cornell, setting this story toward print. My not-so-anonymous readers gave time, insight, and the green light to publish (thank you, Akiko Busch and Roger Panetta). With a deft hand, Michael McGandy at Cornell University Press pushed this book into the world. He is an attentive and sharp editor and made this book infinitely better with his care. Marian

Rogers offered the manuscript a beautiful polish and saved me from my mistakes. The team at Cornell, Susan Specter, Susan Barnett, and Katherine Liu, all made this process a pleasure.

Ucross Foundation supported me with time, space, and great food at a crucial moment in my writing. The wide Wyoming land and sky were space enough to move and think and offered the perfect contrast to tales of the Hudson River. To the staff: you spoiled me. To all of the residents I met while there: you were an inspiration.

Peter Schoenberger lent his photographic talents for the cover of this book, and offered the unexpected gifts of birds and of love in the final months of revision and production.

My niece Alice Debarre wrote to say that she had read my book and thought it was beautiful at a time I needed to hear that. My nephew Thomas carries on his grandfather's kindness and spirit. For both of them I hope this book gives them a view of their American family and lives. To Odette Baczkowski for being the center and soul of Estampes, the place I call home in France, my love.

My sister, Rebecca Rogers, lived this journey with me, sharing in my elation and sadness. Her love brought me through these lonely, beautiful, sad, and wondrous years on the Hudson River.

Lower Navigable Hudson River

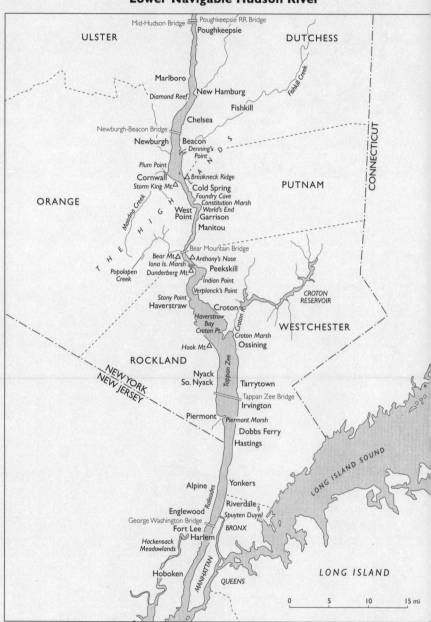